Fontenay

Tilly-sur-
Seulles

Carpiquet

Inf Div

Bretteville
L'Orgeilleuse

River

St-Léger

Creully

Esquay

Bayeux

Courselles

La Rivière

Asnelles

Le Hamel

Arromanches

Port-en-Bessin

0745

MIKE

LOVE

KING

JIG

ITEM

HOW

GEORGE

H-HOUR 0735

G O L D

H-HOUR 0725

Cdn 8 Bde

Cdn 7 Bde

69 Bde

231 Bde

47 RM Cmdos

Cdn 9 Bde

151 Bde

56 Bde

Cdn 3 Inf Div
Cdn 2 Armd Bde

Br 50 Inf Div
Br 8 Armd Bde

Br XXX Corps (Bucknall)

British 2nd Army (Dempsey)

21 Army Group (Montgomery)

6 June 1944

D-DAY

6 June 1944

D-DAY

Over 180 photographs, including some rarely-seen images

Stephen Hart

Published by Amber Books Ltd
United House
London N7 9DP
United Kingdom
www.amberbooks.co.uk
Facebook: amberbooks
YouTube: amberbooksltd
Instagram: amberbooksltd
X(Twitter): @amberbooks

ISBN: 978-1-83886-366-1

Editor: Michael Spilling
Designer: Mark Batley
Picture research: Terry Forshaw

Printed in China

Contents

Introduction

The name 'D-Day' rings out from the pages of history as one of the twentieth century's most momentous days. Designated Operation Neptune/Overlord, D-Day was the common name for the 6 June 1944 Western Allied landings on the well-defended Normandy coast of German-occupied northern France. D-Day was the most important Western Allied operation of World War II in Europe. On that fateful day, the Allies launched the most ambitious amphibious assault seen up to that time. Neptune was the naval operation to transport and land the forces ashore, whereas Overlord involved the subsequent ground and airborne assaults. By the end of D-Day, 157,000 American, British and Canadian ground and airborne troops, plus 177 French commandos, had established major beachheads along the Normandy coast.

In hindsight, such success seemed likely, yet at the time many senior Allied commanders involved were very concerned that enemy resistance might thwart the invasion. The numerous Allied forces committed, the millions of hours of preparatory staff work and training undertaken, and the bravery of thousands of ordinary service personnel transformed the vast challenge that was D-Day into a successful operation. The initial triumph of establishing the Second Front locked Germany into a three-front attritional war – in France, Italy and the East – that would eventually, in May 1945, overwhelm the Nazi German Reich.

The Allied D-Day invasion plan, finalized in February 1944, set its objective as: to assault the Normandy coast and advance inland to secure

BELOW:
MEETING OF THE SURPEME COMMAND
The Allied High Command for D-Day consisted of (from left to right): Lt-Gen Omar Bradley; Admiral Bertram Ramsay; Air Chief Marshal Arthur Tedder; General Eisenhower; General Montgomery; Air Chief Marshal Trafford Leigh-Mallory; and Eisenhower's Chief of Staff, Maj-Gen Walter Beddell Smith.

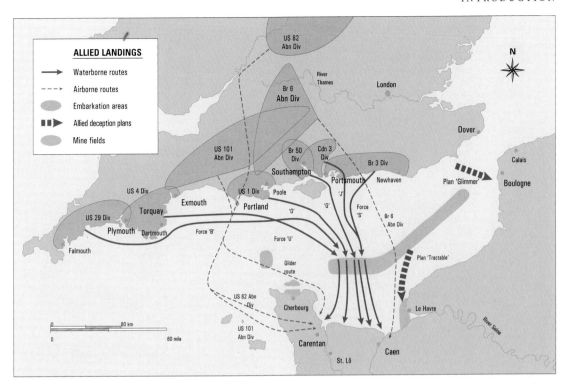

ABOVE:

INVASION PLAN

In the final "Overlord" plan, the two American ground assault groupings departed from the southern ports of Cornwall, Devon and Dorset, while the three British/Canadian ones left from the harbours of Hampshire and Sussex.

as a base for future decisive operations a sizeable Lodgement Area, which by D+90 days would extend to the Loire and Seine rivers. On D-Day, a vast fleet of warships and troop transports would cross the Channel during night-time. Next, around dawn, the fleet would halt offshore opposite the five designated invasion beaches, code named from east to west: Sword, Juno, Gold, Omaha and Utah.

By then, three Allied airborne divisions would have landed to secure the invasion's flanks. Finally, after fierce aerial and naval bombardments, British and Canadian forces would land on Sword, Juno and Gold, while American units assaulted Omaha and Utah.

After these initial assaults had established five small beachheads, follow-up forces would advance inland. By midnight, the Allies hoped that their forces would have captured Caen and Bayeux, as well as consolidated the four eastern beachheads and the British airborne zone into a single salient.

These three beachheads would then be sufficiently resilient to withstand whatever countermeasures the enemy could muster.

BELOW:

INLAND POSITIONS

Allied troops, probably Canadians, collect water from the well of one the villages inland from the Normandy beaches during the expansion of the bridgehead on the afternoon of 6th June 1944.

PREPARATIONS

It was not until 1943 that the Western Allies began to grasp the vast array of preparations they would have to undertake in order to be in a position to contemplate launching a successful amphibious assault of German-occupied Northwest Europe. The mind-bogglingly extensive preparations that the Western Allies had to undertake fell into six main categories. The Allies had to: first, assemble over 2 million fully equipped troops, formed into many dozens of divisions, in southern England; second, decide the most appropriate location to mount the invasion (while successfully deceiving the enemy to expect it would be mounted elsewhere); third, create an appropriate command structure for this multinational tri-service (joint) force; fourth, develop specialized equipment and weaponry to overcome the defenders' inherent combat advantages; fifth, systematically subject the French and Belgian railway network to aerial attack to undermine the German ability to resupply and reinforce their forces that defended the coast of Northwest Europe; and sixth, train many dozens of divisions in unit- and formation-level combined-arms combat.

AMERICAN REDEPLOYMENT

To meet the first requirement, the Western Allies had to redeploy from North America into the United Kingdom 1.3 million troops, and eventually assemble over 2 million troops in hundreds of camps located across central and southern England. Consequently, during 1943–44, hundreds of shipping convoys brought hundreds of thousands of American and Canadian troops, together with weapons and equipment, across the Atlantic to disembark at the UK ports of Belfast, Glasgow, Liverpool, Swansea, Cardiff, Bristol and Plymouth.

OPPOSITE:
ON THE QUAYSIDE
With Landing Ship Tank (LST) US-134 in the background, during 1 June 1944 a US Army GMC CCKW 6x6 cargo truck, fitted with a Browning M2HB heavy machine gun, prepares for embarkation on to an unidentified LST.

LEFT:

FAMILY EVACUATION

During winter 1943–44, families had to evacuate their coastal homes around Slapton Sands in South Devon, England, so that the area – which bore some resemblance to the Normandy coast – could be used for US amphibious assault rehearsals.

OPPOSITE:

ANTI-AIRCRAFT GUNS

At a military depot in southern England during spring 1944, 80 newly produced QF 40mm (1.57in) Mark III ("Bofors") anti-aircraft guns await dispatch to units slated to participate in the D-Day landings.

BELOW:

DARTMOUTH HARBOUR

The American LST US-289 limps into Dartmouth Harbour, South Devon, after being torpedoed by a German S-boat fast attack craft during the April 1944 Exercise Tiger, the full-scale invasion rehearsal at Slapton Sands (80-G-K-2054).

Simultaneously, other British formations were shipped back from the Mediterranean theatre of war to the British Isles.

Once physically located within the UK, these forces had gradually to be concentrated in southern England, and an enormous logistical infrastructure created to resupply them. Thus, by 1 June 1944, there were deployed across southern and central England some 2,034,500 ground force personnel allocated to Overlord, plus the sizeable allocated air force and naval contingents. Although the USA, Britain and Canada provided the bulk of these forces, they were augmented by many smaller contributions. These came from eight European governments in exile after German occupation (Belgium, Czechoslovakia, Denmark, France, Greece, the Netherlands, Norway and Poland) as well as from the Dominions of Australia and New Zealand.

SELECTING A LANDING SITE

Second, the Allies had to select the best location from which to mount the invasion. Many factors influenced this choice – which the Allies eventually decided was Normandy – including: the nature of the enemy coastal defences; the width of the Channel; the cover that could be provided by aerial assets; the suitability of beach terrain; the ease of advance inland; the location of German mobile reserves; the ease of logistical resupply; and the wider geostrategic context.

Having selected the Normandy coast as the location for the landings, the Allies then had to deceive the enemy into expecting it elsewhere. The Allied deception scheme sought to reinforce German

PHOENIX CAISSONS
To increase the supplies delivered into Normandy, the Allies constructed two portable Mulberry harbours that included 136 floating reinforced-concrete Phoenix caissons, which were towed across the Channel and sunk to form these harbours' breakwaters.

misperceptions that the Allies would land at the Pas-de-Calais, where the Channel was at its narrowest. These deception efforts included: the creation of phantom units with dummy vehicles and equipment positioned in Kent under General Patton's command; false intelligence "accidently" leaked to suspected German spies; and copious fake radio traffic. The ruse worked, with many German senior commanders continuing to believe that even after the D-Day landings had occurred, they were merely a feint to draw in German reserves before the "actual" invasion occurred around Calais.

COMMAND STRUCTURE

Third, the Allies had to create an appropriate command hierarchy for what would be one of the most complex multinational joint combined-arms operations ever undertaken. As an interim measure, during 1943, the HQ of the Chief of Staff to Supreme Allied Commander (designate) – COSSAC, one Lt-Gen Frederick Morgan – did the initial invasion planning with the forces of the British 21st Army Group. Next, the Supreme Headquarters Allied Expeditionary Force (SHAEF) become

operational at Bushy Park in London on 12 February 1944. SHAEF was an Anglo-American multinational tri-service HQ. Its commander – the Supreme Commander, Allied Expeditionary Force (SCAEF) – was the American General Dwight (Ike) Eisenhower. Despite his limited operational field command experience, Ike possessed the determination and diplomatic skills required to hold together this at times fragile multinational alliance. To soothe any such inter-Allied tensions, Eisenhower's Deputy SCAEF was the British Air Chief Marshal Arthur Tedder. It was through the latter, moreover, that Ike directed the strategic aerial assets assigned to support (but not be subordinated to) Operation Overlord. These assets belonged to Lt-Gen Carl Spaatz's US Strategic Air Forces Europe and Marshal of the Royal Air Force (RAF) Sir Arthur Harris' Bomber Command.

THEATRE CHIEFS

Below Eisenhower and Tedder came the three senior service theatre chiefs. As Commander-in-Chief Allied Expeditionary Naval Force, the British Admiral Bertram Ramsay controlled

OPPOSITE ABOVE:
FEEDING THE TROOPS
In an unidentified American military camp located somewhere in southwestern England on 22 May 1944, long lines of US soldiers, mess tins clutched in hands, queue to receive some welcome hot food.

OPPOSITE BELOW:
MARCHING TO WAR
On 28 May 1944, a column of British Army soldiers march through an unidentified village street in southern England; they file past a female civilian who is resting her arms on a wheeled cart.

OVERLEAF:
3-D MAP
A group of military personnel and civil servants gather round a table on which is laid a large 3-dimensional map of the Normandy coastline that appears to have been produced using a thick rubber base sheet.

Operation Neptune, the naval dimension of Overlord. As Commander-in-Chief, Allied Expeditionary Air Force, the British Air Chief Marshal Trafford Leigh-Mallory exercized command authority over the 4,176 tactical air platforms allocated to Overlord; these assets were deployed by either the US Ninth Air Force or the RAF's 2nd Tactical Air Force.

Finally, for D-Day itself and the initial land campaign, Eisenhower temporarily delegated his operational control of all ground forces to the British General Bernard Montgomery, commander of the British 21st Army Group. Montgomery, therefore, was in effect a temporary theatre land forces commander. For the Normandy campaign, the 21st Army Group controlled four subordinate army commands, each led by a Lieutenant-General: Miles Dempsey's Second British Army; Omar Bradley's First US Army (FUSA); Henry Crerar's First Canadian Army; and George Patton's Third US Army (TUSA). Dempsey's and Bradley's command were the assault forces, whereas Crerar and Patton's armies were designated as follow-on forces.

SPECIALIZED LANDING CRAFT

Fourth, during 1942–44, the Allies also developed specialized troop-landing vessels and armoured fighting vehicles (AFVs) to increase the likelihood that the D-Day landings would succeed against strong enemy coastal defences. The Allies developed numerous new specialized troop-landing craft, including: Landing Craft, Control (LCC), to function as HQs; Landing Craft, Support (LCS) for fire support; and six Landing Barge variants including field kitchen and drinking-water carriers. In addition, the assault infantry

needed mobile direct-fire AFVs to suppress or destroy the enemy's bunkers. These specialized AFVs included the following vehicles: Duplex Drive (DD) amphibious Sherman tanks; Flail mine-clearing Shermans; US Sherman and British Churchill Crocodile flame-thrower tanks; British Churchill Armoured Vehicles Royal Engineers (AVREs); close support Centaur IVs; and mat-laying, dozer-bladed or fascine-laying Shermans.

TRANSPORTATION PLAN

Fifth, the Allies had to systematically degrade the railway system in France. Ongoing during 1943, these strikes were increased under the Transportation Plan. From 6 March to 10 June 1944, Allied strategic bombers attacked railway junctions, stations, signal boxes, marshalling yards, bridges and repair facilities. These attacks, augmented by Resistance sabotage, were hugely successful. During 6–10 June, 4,700 German trains were halted part-way on their journeys in France; crucially, not a single German military train managed to cross the Loire or Seine into the Normandy battle space.

OPPOSITE ABOVE:
SHERMAN DD TANK
This US Army Sherman DD (Duplex Drive) tank has been outfitted with a snorkel device on its intake and exhaust. This would allow the tank to operate in waves up to 0.3m (1ft) high. Such tanks were designed to propel through the water during the beach assault and provide fire support for the infantry, knocking out German fortified positions on landing. Of the 29 DD tanks launched in the first wave on Omaha Beach, 27 sank before reaching land.

OPPOSITE BELOW:
SHERMAN CRAB FLAIL TANK
During a pre-invasion exercise, a Sherman Crab flail tank – with its turret turned rearwards – uses its rapidly rotating flail device to pound the ground, thus detonating any land mines there present.

FREE FRENCH FORCES
On 31 May 1944, female officers from the Free French Forces, armed with Thompson and Sten submachine guns, participate in weapons training during the final preparations for D-Day.

COMBAT TRAINING

Finally, to be ready to launch D-Day, the Western Allied armies had first to conduct the necessary extensive unit and formation single-arm and combined-arms ground combat training, while the naval and aerial forces conducted their required single-service training regimens. The ground forces' training helped inculcate the troops – many of whom lacked previous combat experience – with the key lessons of modern warfare that had been painfully learned or relearned during the North African and Italian campaigns during 1942–44. The ground troops also had to become skilled in utilizing the new weapons and equipment developed during 1942–44, such as the M4 Sherman tank, the up-gunned Sherman Firefly, the 17-pounder anti-tank gun, or the American Bazooka or British PIAT handheld infantry anti-tank devices.

The ground forces also needed extensive inter-arms training, so that the infantry, for example, could effectively exploit the suppressive effect of artillery indirect fire while simultaneously cooperating tactically with supporting Sherman or Churchill tanks. Furthermore, in addition to extensive training for ground combat, the Allied land forces had to practise the coordination of tactical air support.

TRAINING
British infantry advance during training in May 1944. The central soldier carries a 7.69mm (0.303in) Bren Mark II Light Machine Gun, while the others each sport a Lee Short Magazine Lee Enfield Rifle Mark I No. 4.

TRI-SERVICE COOPERATION

Finally, ground and air units conducted extensive training with amphibious assets, with assault troops rehearsing swift embarkation/disembarkation drills from troop-landing craft. Maritime crews practised convoy formation sailing drills while the fleet's warship and LCS crews practised engaging enemy bunkers. As spring 1944 unfolded, Allied training shifted to tri-service efforts. Ground, air and naval forces learned to work smoothly together, creating the effective tri-service cooperation required for success. Then, during April–May, large-scale Allied amphibious assaults unfolded along the southern English coast. During 22–30 April, in Exercise Tiger, for example, 30,600 US troops assaulted the Devon coast; sadly, a German E-boat incursion sank two vessels, killing 749 Allied personnel.

Thus, by 1 June, the Allies had assembled in southern England a 2 million-strong ground force, equipped it with the necessary equipment, formulated the supporting aerial and naval plans, and trained these forces in single-service and inter-service activity. The Allies were ready to launch D-Day. They now had to select one of the few possible future days in each month when there would be the best mix of permissive moon state (to facilitate airborne drops), timely halfway rising tides (so landing craft could avoid beach obstacles), plenty of daylight (to enable the maximum exploitation) and finally, fair weather with a reasonably calm sea state.

OPPOSITE:
TOMMY GUN
Three British infantrymen – each sporting a M1928A1 Thompson submachine-gun – undertake tactical training in a mock urban environment shortly before the initiation of the D-Day invasion.

ABOVE RIGHT:
UNARMED COMBAT
Just before D-Day, American troops deployed in Devon conduct unarmed combat training; these techniques included eye gouges, jabs to the Adam's apple, and a heel smashed down on a shin.

CANADIAN PARAS
Troops from the 1st Canadian Parachute Battalion, who have been fully kitted-out for combat on D-Day, wait to be transported to RAF Down Ampney airfield, in Wiltshire, on 5 June to embark on their Dakota transports. The unit dropped into Normandy on the morning of the 6th June 1944, and took up positions east of the landing zones.

LANDING SHIPS
Two American Landing Ships, Tank (LSTs), US 314 and US 374, berthed at a pier in a southern English harbour waiting to embark its cargo, while in the foreground are three small Landing Craft, Mechanised (LCMs).

LEFT:
VALENTINE DD TANKS
During Spring 1944, a squadron of British Army Valentine DD tanks have been prepared and readied for amphibious operations, with their rubber and canvas floatation screen positioned all around the vehicle, waiting to be erected. The Valentine was an outdated combat tank, but proved useful for developing and practicing with the DD technology. Valentine tanks were not used on D-Day itself.

OVERLEAF:
SLAPTON SANDS REHEARSAL
Seven LCVPs (Higgins Boats) each bring a platoon to the shore of Slapton Sands, South Devon, during spring 1944; seven amphibian AFVs have already reached the beach, while the small black specks nearby may well be assault infantry.

ABOVE:
PRACTICE RUN
An American army jeep disembarks from a shallow-draught Rhino ferry grounded on the shoreline during an invasion rehearsal held on the southwestern English coast during spring 1944.

RIGHT:
ROLL CALL
This is the last roll call for a company of US soldiers before they board landing craft ready for the big assault on the European continent.

OPPOSITE:
PREPARING TO CROSS
On 1 June 1944, at a southern English harbour, a large landing vessel, probably an LCT, is tied up to the dockside, while in front of it sits an LCVP carrying 20 US soldiers.

GERMAN DEFENCES

Even as major Allied preparations for D-Day unfolded during 1943, German-occupied Northwest Europe remained a strategic backwater. The German Führer, Adolf Hitler, and the High Command both still believed that the Allies were neither psychologically nor materially ready to launch an invasion in the West during that year. The Germans thus only modestly enhanced their "Atlantic Wall" defences, the allegedly formidable fortifications along the Atlantic coast. In reality, though, the Atlantic Wall existed only adjacent to major ports; otherwise, it remained largely a propaganda fiction.

Instead, throughout 1943 the Germans used occupied France as an area to reconstitute formations shattered in the East and to work up new divisions prior to deployment to Russia and (from September 1943) to Italy. The permanent German occupation forces in France thus were low-quality, third-rate coastal defence divisions. Almost no significant operational reserve existed in the West, besides refitting or newly forming mechanized formations. After Hitler had accepted in November 1943 that an Allied invasion would occur during 1944, however, German strategy swiftly prioritized the Western theatre. Over the next seven months, the Wehrmacht (Armed Forces) transferred many veterans and new recruits to the West, as well as numerous modern weapons, including 260 Panther tanks.

OPPOSITE:
FIELD MARSHAL ROMMEL
German Field Marshal Erwin Rommel, commander of Army Group B, inspects a bunker along the Atlantic Wall coastal fortifications that houses what appears to be a 7.5cm (2.95in) PaK 40 anti-tank gun.

ARMOURED RESERVES

This influx of forces meant that by early June 1944 the Germans had established sufficient strength in northern France to stand a very slim chance of thwarting the invasion. To make this remote chance even viable, however, the Germans needed to deduce in advance when and where the Allies would invade. This would allow the Wehrmacht swiftly to commit its armoured reserves to ripostes that might throw the Allies, when still not yet firmly established ashore, back into the sea.

However, some key commanders, including General Leo Geyr von Schweppenburg, instead myopically wanted to husband the mobile reserves for decisive action later in the campaign.

Yet even the Germans' very remote chance of success on D-Day was hampered by their inadequate logistics, which, when further degraded by Allied aerial strikes, meant that the Germans lacked the supplies required for sustained operations. The only chance for German victory existed on 6 June.

This remote chance of German ground force success on D-Day also required that their over-matched air force and navy somehow disrupt Allied mastery of the skies and seas.

In hindsight, it is now clear that if the Germans failed to repel D-Day during its first day, the likelihood of German strategic victory in the West plummeted from extremely unlikely to impossible.

DIGGING A WEAPONS PIT
The crew of a German 15cm (5.9in) artillery piece dig a weapons pit from which they will fire their gun. German guns of this calibre had a typical maximum firing range of 24.5km (15 miles).

GERMAN NAVAL AND AIR FORCE STRENGTH

In addition to commanding the German ground forces in Northwest Europe, Field Marshal Gerd von Rundstedt's tri-service Supreme Command West (SCW) also theoretically controlled the German Air Force (Luftwaffe) and Naval (Kriegsmarine) High Commands West; in practice, both these service commands enjoyed significant autonomy. Both of these commands, moreover, were utterly overshadowed by the opposing Allied aerial and naval contingents; they struggled to provide the defending German ground forces with the joint support they required.

The German naval contingents based in the Channel ports merely consisted of a small number of minor assets, including E-boat and S-boat attack craft, plus a few submarines. These were unlikely to significantly disrupt the execution of Operation Neptune.

Similarly, General of Flyers Hugo Sperrle's Air Fleet III had just 400 operational fighters on strength, and most of these were committed to intercepting en route the hundreds of Allied strategic bombers that daily attacked targets in Germany.

The aerial countermeasures executed by Sperrle's fighters only managed to retard very marginally the Allied aerial bombing onslaught against French transport networks initiated in the Transportation Plan.

GROUND FORCES STRENGTH

On 6 June, Field Marshal von Rundstedt's SCW controlled, in addition to its naval and aerial forces, three chief subordinate ground commands: Field Marshal Erwin Rommel's Army Group B; Col-Gen Blaskowitz's Army Group G; and General Leo Geyr von Schweppenburg's Armoured Group West. Between them, these commands controlled 53 titular divisions, including 44 infantry-style divisions and nine mobile formations.

On 31 May 1944, Supreme Command West deployed 1,811 AFVs, including: 1,355 combat tanks (namely, 759 Panzer IVs and 543 Panther medium tanks, as well as 53 Tiger I and five King Tiger heavy tanks); 345 StuG III and IV assault guns; 204 Jagdpanzer IV, IV/70 and V tank destroyers; and 112 assorted other AFVs.

These forces were primarily fielded by SCW's nine mobile formations, namely five Army and three Waffen-SS armoured (panzer) divisions plus one Waffen-SS panzergrenadier (mechanized) division. These nine divisions formed the backbone of the German defensive efforts to stymie the Allied Second Front. These elite mobile formations fielded the best personnel and had considerably higher equipment levels than the typical German infantry-style divisions.

OPPOSITE ABOVE:
FIGHTER PILOT
Crewmen attend to a German Messerschmitt Bf 109 fighter pilot. During D-Day the Luftwaffe managed just 210 Focke Wulf Fw 190 fighter sorties against the Allied forces, whereas total Allied aerial sorties that day were 14,600.

OPPOSITE BELOW:
CONSTRUCTION WORK
Organisation Todt workers utilize large cement mixers while constructing a coastal artillery battery during October 1943; although unfinished by D-Day, the Atlantic Wall had already consumed some 17 million cubic metres (600 million cubic feet) of concrete.

LEFT:
FIELD MARSHAL VON RUNDSTEDT
During a visit to the Atlantic Wall on 18 April 1944, the German Supreme Commander West, Field Marshal Gerd von Rundstedt, discusses troop movement with what appears to be an armoured unit officer.

OPPOSITE:
PROPAGANDA
This Nazi propaganda image from June 1944 shows a company of German soldiers marching briskly past a substantial bunker area somewhere on the Atlantic Wall in Northern France.

BELOW:
CONSTRUCTING DEFENCES
This photograph taken on 26 April 1944 shows the ongoing construction work underway at an uncompleted part of the Atlantic Wall coastal fortifications near Saint-Malo harbour, located on Brittany's northern coast.

BIG GUN
The most powerful German coastal artillery pieces deployed along the Atlantic Wall were typically situated in large casemates of reinforced concrete, like this one in the Bay of Biscay.

LXXXVI CORPS NORMANDY DEPLOYMENT

Rommel's Army Group B controlled northern France and Belgium while Army Group G controlled southern France. Army Group B fielded two armies: Col-Gen Friedrich Dollmann's Seventh Army controlled Northwest France (Brittany and Normandy down to the River Loire); and the Fifteenth Army controlled northeastern France (including the Pas-de-Calais) and Belgium.

Within the Seventh Army, Artillery General Marcks' LXXXVI Corps defended the Calvados and Manche coasts, along which the Allied onslaught would unfold. On D-Day, Marcks' Corps fielded six infantry divisions, one of which – the 319th – was fixed in defence of the Channel Islands. Four of these formations – the 243rd, 319th, 709th and 716th – were second-rate static infantry divisions, with just the 91st and 352nd divisions being first-rate field infantry formations. The 716th Division, on the Corps' east, defended the coast from the Dives estuary westwards to Port-en-Bessin (where the Sword, Juno and Gold assaults would occur). Next, the 352nd Division defended the coast westwards to the Baie des Veys at the base of the

Cotentin Peninsula; the 709th Division manned the Cotentin's eastern coast, with the 243rd and 91st divisions defending the peninsula's northern and western coasts, respectively. Although declared an army group reserve, 21st Panzer Division units were also sited within the Corps' area.

FORMATION STRENGTHS

These defending German formations and units had official War Establishments that stated their authorized personnel and equipment strengths. Many formations in Normandy, however, had actual strengths below their authorized levels, utilized sundry captured enemy weapons, and/ or also had elements configured differently from the official War Establishments.

In June 1944, the Establishment strength of a 1944 Model first-rate field infantry division (such as the 352nd deployed against Omaha Beach) was 12,500 personnel.

In addition, the authorized strength of a Model 1944 German Army (rather than Waffen-SS) panzer division was 14,787 men together with 79 Mark V Panther and 101 Panzer IV tanks, plus 30 Panzerjäger IV tank destroyers or StuG III/IV assault guns. These Model 1944 panzer divisions comprised an armoured regiment, two armoured-infantry (panzergrenadier) regiments, an artillery regiment, a reconnaissance and anti-tank battalion, and supporting signals, engineer, flak, transport and supply units.

The nine mobile divisions – eight panzer divisions and one mechanized (panzergrenadier) division – deployed in the West during June 1944 were the key force with which the German high command hoped to repel any Allied invasion.

OPPOSITE ABOVE:
ANTI-TANK DITCH
The German forces defending the Normandy coast constructed V-shaped concrete-lined anti-tank ditches to prevent Allied armour from moving inland; this particular ditch was located near Ouistreham.

OPPOSITE BELOW:
KEEPING WATCH
A German sentry standing by the shore, and equipped with a Kar 98k rifle, scans the sea's horizon for any signs of Allied ships; this would indicate that the long-awaited Allied invasion of France had begun.

BEACH OBSTACLES
Expecting that the Allied assault would occur at high tide, when the width of the beach "killing area" was minimized, the Germans emplaced explosive-laden obstacles like these; as landing craft sailed in at high tide, their undersides would hit the obstacle and be sunk by the resulting explosion.

AT THE SHARP END

Yet the bulk of the German resistance offered during D-Day would come from three of Marcks' five infantry divisions. In terms of rifleman bayonet strength, the German Model 1944 infantry division fielded three two-battalion Grenadier regiments, each of 1,997 troops. This gave the division an establishment bayonet strength of eighteen 142-person rifle companies, giving a total of 2,556 infanteers. These three regiments, moreover, each also sported three heavy companies and three anti-tank companies of infanteers equipped respectively with field and anti-tank guns.

The main German infantry weapon was the MG42 machine gun, of which each infantry company deployed 15 (with a further nine in the regimental support companies). The nine-person German rifle section existed to service and protect the automatic fire-effect of the formidable MG42. With well-drilled crews stocked with 250-round ammunition belts and able to swiftly exchange overheating barrels, an MG42 could deliver sustained fire of 200 rpm and shorter bursts of up to 500 rpm. This lethal weapon exerted a significant suppressive effect on assaulting Allied troops.

ABOVE:
MG42
Young German soldiers man an MG42 heavy machine gun somewhere along the French coast, 1944. These soldiers are also equipped with a bunch of Stielhandgranate stick grenades (foreground).

The rest of the German section was equipped with the 1935-designed 7.92mm (0.31in) Kar 98k bolt-action rifle. The 33-man German infantry platoon also fielded four light-role (bipod-mounted) MG42s, a 5cm (1.96in) mortar, and several Panzerfaust-held infantry anti-tank devices.

ARTILLERY BATTERIES & STRONGPOINTS

The effect of these German weapons and their survivability were enhanced because most were sited in well-established positions within the Atlantic Wall coastal defences. Despite already using 17 million cubic metres (600 million cubic feet) of concrete, the Germans, however, were still in the process of constructing the Wall's artillery fortifications and strongpoints when D-Day occurred.

The most potent of these defences were a few coastal heavy artillery batteries – usually adjacent to key ports like Cherbourg and Le Havre – that mounted large-calibre, long-range guns. East of Cherbourg, for example, Batterie Hamburg fielded four 24cm (9.4in) SK L/40 naval guns with a maximum range of 26.6km

OPPOSITE:
S-BOATS IN THE CHANNEL
The S-Boat fast attack craft, based at Cherbourg and le Havre, played some part in the meagre German maritime response to D-Day; such vessels had a top speed of 36 knots and typically sported 50cm (19.7 inch) torpedo tubes and a 20mm (0.8 inch) cannon.

(16.5 miles). The powerful Batterie Todt, at Cap Gris-Nez (near Calais), moreover, sported four 38cm (15in) SK C/34 battleship guns with a range of up to 55.7km (34.6 miles). The Germans had also established many additional batteries with medium-calibre weapons. The Batterie Longues-sur-Mer, located between Gold and Omaha beaches, for example, sported four M272 bunkers that each housed a 15cm (5.9in) TbtsK C/36 naval gun that had a maximum range of 14.5km (14.6 miles).

RESISTANCE NESTS

The Atlantic Wall also comprised many hundreds of coastal Resistance Nest strongpoints, such as WN62, which covered Omaha Beach. These strongpoints each typically sported a bunker that housed their primary weapon, often either an 8.8cm (3.4in) Flak gun, a 7.5cm (2.9in) Pak 40 anti-tank gun, or an ex-Belgian 7.5cm (2.9in) FK235b field cannon. Pairs of these guns typically established interlocking arcs of enfilade fire along the beaches across which the assaulting Allied troops would advance. A Resistance Nest was usually defended by an infantry company from the infantry division allocated that sector of the coast, although larger strongpoints housed either a naval or army coastal artillery battery.

Most infantry Resistance Nests also had four or five concrete emplacements that sported various support weapons, including: tripod-mounted MG42 heavy machine guns; a 5cm (1.96in) GW 36 or GW 201f mortar; a captured French Renault tank turret mounting a 5cm (1.96in) KwK L/42 ex-tank cannon; and several flamethrowers.

Some 104 Resistance Nests or larger batteries defended the Normandy coast where the five Allied invasion assaults would occur. The existence of these incomplete Atlantic Wall defences made the Allied task of successfully securing beachheads on D-Day much more challenging.

ABOVE:
RESISTANCE NEST
German soldiers man fortifications on the Atlantic Wall, April 1944. The artillery piece appears to be a medium calibre, possibly a 7.5cm (2.9in).

OPPOSITE ABOVE:
LARGE-CALIBRE ARTILLERY
Some German fortifications along the French coast, like this sentry guarded one, sported large-calibre artillery guns: near Cherbourg, for example, Batterie Hamburg fielded four 24cm (9.5in) SK L/40 pieces.

OPPOSITE LEFT & RIGHT:
OBSERVATION POSTS
Along the Atlantic Wall, the Germans constructed numerous observation posts; due to the earth's curvature, a soldier standing at sea level can only see 5km (3 miles) out to sea, whereas at a 10m (33ft) height, an observer can see 11km (7 miles).

RIGHT:
COASTAL DEFENCES
Profile view of German defences
built into the sloping ground
above an invasion beach; in
the centre distance, out at sea,
large spouts of water can be
seen, presumably caused by
the detonation of large-calibre
German coastal artillery rounds.

BELOW:
DRAGON'S TEETH
The defending German forces
established in many coastal areas
zones of reinforced-concrete
square-pyramidal "Dragon's
Teeth" anti-tank obstacles, in
an attempt to prevent Allied
AFVs that had landed from
advancing inland.

LEFT:
NEBELWERFER
The Nebelwerfer were a family of multi-barrelled indirect-fire rocket-launcher systems, which the Germans utilised in Normandy to mitigate their limited artillery capabilities. The Germans used "shoot and scoot" tactics with these weapons, moving them once fired between multiple pre-prepared firing-pits to avoid their destruction by Allied counter-measures.

BELOW:
BUNKER
In the background, jutting out from the sea wall, a German bunker houses either a 75mm (2.95in) or 88mm (3.46in) anti-tank gun; rather than face out to sea, the gun enjoys increased protection when configured to fire enfilade along the beach.

BEHIND ENEMY LINES

Another force multiplier that the invading Allied forces strove to exploit, to boost the chances that the D-Day landings would succeed, was to utilize the French Resistance to disrupt the defending German forces. The term "French Resistance" was a generic catch-all name for the numerous movements that mounted their own struggles against German occupation (and until November 1942, against the German puppet collaborationist Vichy regime in southern France). Some of the key Resistance groups included: the Gaullist/Free French Central Bureau of Intelligence and Operations; the National Resistance Council; the Communist French Francs-Tireurs and Partisans; and various Maquisard rural guerrilla bands.

Resistance activists across Western Europe had already played a significant part in preparations for Operation Overlord. Throughout 1942–44, French citizens had covertly gathered many thousands of pieces of intelligence. Civilian clerks working in German military HQs, for example, had surreptitiously reproduced, photographed or copied by hand thousands of German documents and passed them on to Resistance networks. Similarly, locals covertly sketched out the layout of German defences or noted down evidence of German force strengths.

OPPOSITE:
ENTENTE
Some weeks after the Normandy bridgehead was secured, Supreme Allied Commander General Dwight Eisenhower, with bespectacled First US Army Commander Omar Bradley just visible behind him, talks to a young member of the French Resistance in Normandy.

Subsequently, late on 1 June 1944, the BBC Overseas Service broadcast the first three lines of Paul Verlaine's famous 1866 poem entitled "Chanson d'automne" ("Autumn Song"). This was a coded message for the French Resistance, informing them that the invasion would take place within the next 14 days. The covert message also instructed the Resistance to step up their sabotage activities against the French railways. German counterintelligence officers soon detected the message and correctly guessed at least some of its significance; but these officers struggled to get higher commanders to heed these warnings.

"CHANSON D'AUTOMNE"

Eventually, on 5 June at 2315 hrs British Double Summer Time (namely, GMT plus two hours), the BBC broadcast the final three lines of Verlaine's poem. This coded message informed the Resistance that D-Day would commence within 48 hours and requested that they begin widespread sabotage attacks. On 6 June itself, French Resistance activists carried out some 996 sabotage strikes against German targets, including railway lines and associated signals equipment, road bridges, overhead power cables, field telephone wires, fuel depots and ammunition dumps.

TERRAIN GUIDES

The Resistance also undertook other supporting activities before and during D-Day. Dozens of operatives risked death, entering the combat zone during 6 June to reach the invading forces, so that they could act as terrain guides for the Allies. The Resistance, at Allied behest, also persuaded many

RAILWAY SABOTAGE
A group of five French Resistance fighters sabotage a railway line located in the district of Saône-et-Loire, between Lyon and Dijon in central-eastern France, during the first week of September 1944.

villagers and farm residents across Normandy to surreptitiously take their dogs inside the home at night, rather than leaving them in garden sheds as usual. This ensured that when Allied airborne troops landed in the early hours of D-Day, their presence would not be inadvertently revealed by barking dogs. As we shall see, this ruse worked well at Gonneville-en-Auge around 0215 hrs on 6 June, when 9 British Paras silently marched through the hamlet undisturbed on their way to assault the German artillery battery at Merville, which threatened the Sword Beach landings.

In the ensuing weeks of the Normandy campaign, moreover, 93 parachute-inserted Anglo-American Jedburgh three-man teams, plus 117 French Free Army paratroopers, assisted the Resistance's subversive activities. These involved continuing sabotage operations, hampering the forward movement of enemy reserves and even mounting local short-term rural guerrilla warfare.

OPPOSITE:
COMBAT
During the German occupation of France, brave activists operating printing machines in secret cellars, like this one, or lofts, clandestinely produced many tens of thousands of copies of the official French Resistance newspaper, *Combat*.

BELOW:
LOCAL KNOWLEDGE
On 7 June 1944 at Surrain, just inland from Omaha Beach, a 50-year-old French farm worker, Gustave Joret, passes information to an American lieutenant from V Corps' Civil Affairs team.

LEFT:
WESTLAND LYSANDER
Due to its ability to take off
from short, grassy, improvised
airstrips, the Westland Lysander
was the preferred British aerial
asset for making clandestine
night flights into German-
occupied Europe, often carrying
parachute canisters.

BELOW:
SUPPLY DROP
Unseen Allied aircraft drop at
least 13 parachute canisters that
contain vital supplies of weapons
and ammunition to a French
Resistance group in Normandy
sometime during June 1944.

LEFT:
LONDON CALLING
French Resistance operatives listened on hidden radios to coded messages aired via the BBC Overseas Service; the reciting of Paul Verlaine's poem "Chanson d'automne" informed the operatives that the invasion was imminent.

BELOW:
CAPTIVE
Seemingly jubilant pistol-toting French Resistance fighters march an anxious German soldier into captivity during June 1944; the prisoner appears to be wearing a Luftwaffe paratrooper jump smock.

NEPTUNE: THE NAVAL OPERATION

During Operation Neptune on 5–6 June, the maritime phase of D-Day, Ramsay commanded a vast fleet of 6,939 vessels. This floating behemoth comprised 1,213 warships, 4,126 troop-landing craft, 726 ancillary vessels and 864 merchant ships; it was one of the largest naval armadas ever employed in war. However, it had been back on 8 May 1944 that Eisenhower had scheduled the D-Day landings to occur on 5 June. This date was one of just three during that month when there existed the required optimal combination of copious moonlight, halfway rising tides soon after dawn and plenty of daylight: the unpredictable factor, of course, remained the weather (and thus the sea state).

The first phase of this intended 5 June D-Day operation unfolded during 2–3 June. Five naval bombardment groups headed south along the British coast from the ports of Belfast, the Clyde and Glasgow, and Scapa Flow in the Orkneys. Each bombardment group would support the assault mounted on one of the five Allied invasion beaches. Simultaneously, on 2 June, two British X-craft midget submarines sailed across the Channel and remained submerged off the Normandy coast: their job was to steer the Allied naval armada into its correct positions.

OPPOSITE:
OFFICIAL BLESSING
A clergyman delivers a sermon on a naval vessel before it heads for the Normandy coast. The Allied high command often employed religious themes in their speeches to the troops, stressing that they were on a Holy "Crusade" to defeat the monstrous evil of Nazism.

HMS *BULOLO*
A British Royal Navy gunner prepares ammunition for his 40mm (1.57in) Bofors anti-aircraft gun aboard HMS *Bulolo* (Landing Ship HQ) off Gold Beach, June 1944.

POSTPONEMENT

Unfortunately, on 4 June, rapidly deteriorating weather
forced Eisenhower to take a colossal decision: reluctantly,
he postponed by 24 hours the D-Day operation slated
for 5 June. This decision both condemned those soldiers
already embarked to an unpleasant night aboard yawing
transport vessels and risked compromising the security
of this top-secret operation. If continuing bad weather
had postponed the invasion beyond 7 June, however, the
Allies would have had to wait two weeks until satisfactory
conditions re-occurred. This would have been a
dangerous delay given that the Germans were then rapidly
strengthening their defences in Normandy.

During the night of 4–5 June, the storm worsened,
but at this dismal moment Allied meteorologists
predicted that better weather would unfold during 6 June.
Consequently, at 0400 hrs on 5 June, Eisenhower took
an eye-wateringly courageous decision: the Allies would
indeed initiate the invasion during 6 June, even though
this would be in sea state and weather conditions much
worse than those for which they had planned. Eisenhower
had just taken a huge gamble, on which so many profound
strategic consequences now hung.

TROOP TRANSPORTATION FLEET

To transport 132,000 assault troops across the Channel the
Allies had assembled a vast maritime troop-transportation
fleet. This comprised 4,126 vessels, including 2,468
landing craft spanning 46 separate designs, some of which
had been specifically constructed for D-Day. The fleet had
five Landing Ships, Headquarters (LSHQs), each one of
which had a tri-service operations room to control activity
on each invasion beach.

COAST GUARD LANDING CRAFT

This Landing Craft, Vehicle, Personnel (LCVP), crewed by the
US Coast Guard, carries infantry to one of the two American
Normandy invasion beaches on D-Day.

ABOVE:
ARMOURED DOZER
On 3 June 1944, an American D6 armoured dozer reverses up the ramp of the Royal Navy's LCT 789 in preparation for sailing across the English Channel on D-Day.

LEFT:
FIREFLY EMBARKS
A Sherman Firefly Mark Vc of the 1st East Riding Yeomanry (from 27th Armoured Brigade), backs on to a LST; the Firefly's potent 17-pounder gun had a lethality superior to that of the German Tiger I tank.

OPPOSITE:
FULLY LOADED
In early June, an assortment of Allied trucks and vehicles have been tightly packed on to a large landing vessel, ready to sail south across the English Channel on D-Day.

LANDING CRAFT, FLAK PLATFORM
Royal Navy Landing Craft, Flak, Vessel LCF 3, a converted
Mark III LCT with its interior decked-over, on which were
mounted four 2-pounder (40mm, 1.57in) and eight 20mm
(0.78in) anti-aircraft guns.

The fleet also included 311 Landing Ships, Tank (LSTs), each of which transported up to 18 tanks, and 768 Landing Craft, Tank (LCTs), each of which could carry up to 11 tanks. Key infantry-carrying assets included the 48 Landing Ships, Infantry (LSIs), each of which transported between 150 and 1,500 soldiers, depending on the design. The fleet also fielded 248 Landing Craft, Infantry (LCIs), of varying designs that could carry 180–210 troops.

In addition, the Allies utilized several thousand small troop-carrying craft, including 640 British 32-troop carrying Landing Craft, Assault (LCAs) and 839 American 36-man carrying Landing Craft, Vehicle, Personnel (LCVPs). This fleet also deployed 15 different types of support craft designs, including fire support vessels, such as Landing Craft, Tank Rocket (LCT-Rs) and air defence assets, such as Landing Craft, Flak (LCFs).

FIRE SUPPORT AND PROTECTION

To protect these 4,126 transport vessels from enemy threats, as well as provide fire support for the beach assaults, the Allies had assembled a fleet of 1,213 warships. This force included: seven battleships (four British Royal Navy and three American); two British 38cm (15in) gunned monitors; five heavy cruisers (two British and three American); 18 light cruisers (including two Free French, one Polish and 15 British vessels); 105 destroyers; 63 frigates and escorts; 71 corvettes; and some 287 minesweepers.

Throughout 5 June, this 6,939-vessel armada had gradually assembled at and adjacent to the harbours of England's southern coast. Under Ramsay's command, this fleet was split into two main commands: American Rear Admiral Alan Kirk's Western Task Force and British Rear

Admiral Philip Vian's Eastern Task Force. Kirk's command consisted of the transport vessels of Assault Forces "U" and "O", slated to operate at Utah and Omaha beaches, respectively. Assault Forces "U" and "O" were each supported by a similarly titled naval Bombardment Group, built around a battleship such as USS *Nevada* or USS *Texas*.

CONVOY RENDEZVOUS

During 2100–2300 hrs on 5 June, the Western Task Force – plus Bombardment Groups "U" and "O" – put to sea from the Devonshire ports of Salcombe, Dartmouth and Brixham, as well as Dorset's Portland, Weymouth and Poole harbours. Simultaneously, the Eastern Task Force, with Assault Forces "S", "J" and "G", plus Bombardment Groups "S", "J" and "G", departed from the Hampshire harbours of Southampton and Portsmouth, and the Sussex ports of Newhaven and Shoreham. An hour later, follow-up convoys departed from Cornwall's Falmouth and Plymouth harbours and from Felixstowe in Suffolk, as well as Harwich and Southend in Essex. Subsequently, the various naval convoys rendezvoused in a large area centred on "Point Z" (or "Piccadilly Circus"), a map-point located 30km (19 miles) southeast of the eastern Isle of Wight. By this time, 238 Allied minesweepers had already steamed south and begun sweeping 10 slightly diverging, marked north–south channels clear of enemy mines, two for each of the five invasion beaches; the area within this cleared area was termed "The Spout".

OPPOSITE:
INVASION FLEET
This photograph, taken from the Baltimore class heavy cruiser USS *Quincy* (CA-71) on the late morning of 6 June, shows elements of the vast Allied invasion fleet operating offshore from Utah Beach.

LEFT:
SHORE BOMBARDMENT
HMS *Belfast* fires during the pre-assault bombardment of the Normandy coast. At 0530 hrs on 6 June, *Belfast* opened fire on a German artillery battery at Ver-sur-Mer on Gold Beach.

LANDING CRAFT FLOTILLA
A convoy of at least 15 Landing Craft, Infantry (Large) approaches the Normandy coast on D-Day; each vessel tows a barrage balloon for protection against low-flying German aircraft.

Subsequently, during the night – between 2330 hrs on 5 June and 0500 hrs on 6 June – this 6,939-vessel armada steamed south across the Channel towards the Normandy coast. By 0500 hrs, as the Allied airborne operations continued to unfold inland, the lead Allied ships had approached the coast, just as the first hints emerged of the lifting of the hitherto shrouding darkness. Around 0505 hrs, several highly attentive German naval observers in elevated observation posts spotted the lead vessels as barely visible specks on the extreme horizon at a distance of around 18.5km (11.5 miles).

Over the next 80 minutes, depending on which was the target beach, the armada's vessels completed their planned steaming south and halted, at a range of between 4 and 12 nautical miles off the coast. To the enemy, the sight of such a vast fleet stretching for as far as the eye could see was utterly shocking. All that Lieutenant Frerking at Strongpoint WN62 on Omaha Beach could do was mumble to himself in disbelief; what he could see was impossible, as there were not that many ships in the entire world. Meanwhile, during 0335–0515 hrs, 1,912 Allied strategic and medium bombers had attacked enemy positions along the Normandy coast and the adjacent hinterland.

COASTAL BOMBARDMENT

At 0520 hrs, the warships stationed northeast of Sword Beach engaged the enemy's coastal defences around Ouistreham. The 38cm (15in) guns of the battleship HMS *Warspite* and the

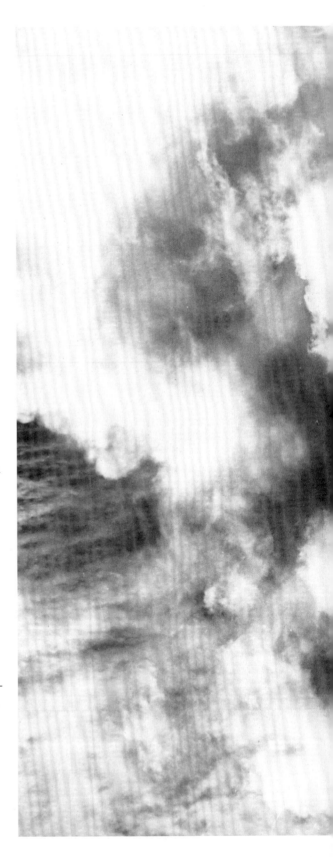

USS *NEVADA*
The five barrels sported by the two forward 35.6cm (14in) gun turrets of the American battleship USS *Nevada* (BB-36) engage the German artillery battery at Saint-Marcouf during the D-Day landings on Utah Beach.

monitor HMS *Roberts* rained down destruction, before being joined by the fire of the Group's five cruisers and 15 destroyers. Next, at 0530 hrs, Bombardment Groups "J" and "G" engaged the enemy defences at Juno and Gold beaches, respectively. Finally, at 0550 hrs, the Western Task Force's two Bombardment Groups engaged the German positions at Omaha and Utah beaches. These ferocious bombardments continued until just a few minutes after the beach assaults were initiated; in the bombardment's final minutes, LCSs and LCT-Rs joined in the barrage.

The five beach assaults then commenced pretty much as scheduled. The precise timings of each depended on the tidal conditions at each locality. Thus, the first Allied beach assaults, those on Utah and Omaha, commenced at 0630 hrs; two other beach assaults, Sword and Gold, followed at 0726 hrs, before the Juno assault was initiated at 0745 hrs. Subsequently, these warships – as we shall see – continued to engage enemy targets as the D-Day assaults and follow-up operations unfolded on 6 June.

ABOVE:
APPROACHING THROUGH THE DAWN
British LCTs carry troops across the Channel as the invasion fleet closes on the Normandy landing sites, morning of 6 June 1944.

TOP:
TRANSPORTING THE WOUNDED
On the afternoon of D-Day, British troops wounded during the assault on Sword Beach are taken on board the heavy cruiser HMS *Frobisher*, which had participated in the pre-assault bombardment of the German defences.

OPPOSITE:
SURVIVOR
A survivor is pulled aboard an American vessel after his landing craft was hit by German artillery fire off a Normandy invasion beach on the morning of 6 June 1944 (US Coast Guard Collection).

RIGHT:
HMS *BELFAST*

The gun-crew of the light cruiser HMS *Belfast* operate its "A" Turret, which mounted three 152mm (6in) Mark XXIII guns, during the bombardment of enemy defences prior to the amphibious assault; note the spent main armament gun cartridges littering the deck.

BELOW:
BIG GUNS

The barrel length of the 152mm (6in) L/50 guns mounted on HMS *Belfast* is illustrated by the gaggle of gun-crew situated beneath this one; the crew all wear anti-flash, fire-resistant protective clothing in case there is a flash-blast of ammunition in the turret's magazine.

ABOVE:
FORWARD GUN TURRETS
View of the starboard (right) side portion of the two forward turrets on HMS *Belfast*, both of which mounted three Mark XXIII guns. Commissioned in August 1939 as part of the Town class, HMS *Belfast* displaced 10,759 tonnes (10,590 tons).

RIGHT:
BATTLE STATIONS
Crew aboard one of a line of British destroyers keep watch. The Allies deployed more than 100 destroyers to provide a protective screen across the English Channel in order to deal with any U-boat or S-boat attacks on the invasion fleet. In the event, four German torpedo boats launched 15 torpedoes against the Eastern Task Force, sinking the Norwegian destroyer *Svenner* off Sword Beach.

ABOVE:

HMS *RODNEY*

Stationed off Sword Beach, the Royal Navy battleship *Rodney* bombarded Bénerville Battery as well as several German positions around Caen with its 406mm (15.98in) main guns.

LEFT:

HMS *WARSPITE*

Warspite was apparently the first battleship to open fire on D-Day, at 0530 hrs, bombarding the Villerville and Mont Canisy batteries off Sword Beach with its 381mm (15in) shells, firing more than 300 in 48 hours.

NAVAL ARTILLERY SPOTTER
Artillery spotters were parachuted into Normandy to guide naval gun
fire at shore targets on D-Day. This British observer is working from
Ouistreham lighthouse, on the far flank of the Sword landing zone.

THE AIRBORNE ASSAULT

From 2245 hrs on 5 June, as the Allied naval armada congregated in the waters around the Isle of Wight, many hundreds of transport planes began to take off from air bases located across southern England. From airfields that ranged east-northeast from Exeter through to Newbury, aircraft took off that transported the first waves of the American 82nd and 101st Airborne Divisions; these formations flew southeast to cross the English coast around Portland. Meanwhile, the transport aircraft carrying the troops of the British 6th Airborne Division took off from airfields in the area between Swindon and Southampton. With further waves of transport aircraft taking off during 6 June itself, by midnight on D-Day some 22,000 airborne troops had been inserted into Normandy.

This mighty air assault was intended to achieve four things: it increased the number of Allied troops that could be inserted into the theatre on 6 June during that critical first day; it widened and deepened the Allied beachhead, dispersing the concentration of enemy forces; through seizing key bridges, it protected the approaches to the eastern and western flanks of the British and American beachheads, respectively; and it also disrupted the likely German armoured responses.

PRACTICE JUMP
American paratroopers make
a mass jump during training in
southern England, early 1944.

LEFT:

READY TO BOARD

A "stick" of heavily encumbered paratroopers from the US 101st Airborne Division wait to board their Douglas C-47 Skytrain transport aircraft on the early evening of 5 June 1944.

OPPOSITE:

COMBAT HAIRCUT

US paratroopers prepare to go into combat by having their heads shaved; some sport a "Mohican"-style strip of hair, presumably in some sort of evocation of the warrior ethos often associated with historical Indigenous Americans.

BELOW:

HAMILCAR GLIDERS

Many rows of paired Hamilcar gliders stand on the runway of an unidentified airfield in southern England, while their four-engined Handley Page Halifax bomber towing aircraft stand at the ready to either side.

ABOVE:

INSIDE A C-47

American 101st Airborne paratroopers seated along both sides of the interior of their C-47 aircraft as it flies towards Normandy; one understandably anxious paratrooper is smoking a calming cigarette.

LEFT:

BOARDING

Three 101st Airborne Division paratroopers wait to board their transport aircraft on the evening of 5 June. Note that they are very heavily weighed down with parachutes, Bergen rucksacks, personal weapons and other combat essentials.

ABOVE:
WAITING TO JUMP
This view of three American paratroopers standing, and clinging firmly on inside their C-47 Skytrain ably illuminates the interior's sectional construction; this four-crew transport aircraft could carry 27 troops.

By 0005 hrs on 6 June, the 821 transport planes loaded with American paratroopers plus a further 96 transports towing Horsa and Waco gliders began forming up in "Vic-of-Vic" formations south of the English coast. On board were some 13,000 troops of the US 82nd and 101st Airborne Divisions. Their missions were to seize key bridges and road junctions and thus both delay German counter-attacks and facilitate the Allied advance from Utah Beach. This aerial armada flew west-southwest until it was just to the north of the Channel Island of Guernsey; here, the formations split. The platforms transporting 82nd Division assets headed east-southeast for a further 82km (51 miles) before crossing over the western coastline of the Cotentin Peninsula around Barneville-Carteret; their story is continued a little later. Meanwhile, the remaining aircraft, carrying the 101st Division's troops, headed 89km (55 miles) southeast until they were just a few miles short of the Cotentin Peninsula's western coast around Portbail.

SCREAMING EAGLES LAND

Here, the aircraft "Vics" turned a little to the left, heading east as they crossed over on to the base of the peninsula. As the transport aircraft dropped down in height, they soon encountered dense clouds as well as intense fire from enemy flak guns. With the pilots forced immediately to take violent evasive action, the "Vic" formations soon broke up into a chaotic mass. Once over the Cotentin's southeastern corner, the sticks of 10

paratroopers began to drop, as gliders silently hurtled to earth at 97km/h (60mph). Each of the 101st Division's three Parachute Infantry Regiments (PIRs), plus supporting elements, were supposed to arrive on or close to Drop-Zones (DZs) A, C and D.

These DZs stretched for 9km (6 miles) in a line from north to south between the flooded valley of the Douve and Merderet rivers, to the west, and the inundated marshlands behind Utah Beach, to the east. Instead, the Division's forces arrived in the theatre very widely dispersed. Although a reasonable concentration was achieved at DZ-C, many of the troops slated to arrive on DZ-A and DZ-D overshot to the north and east. Most of those destined for DZ-D actually landed just to the south and southeast of DZ-C, between Vierville-sur-Mer and Sainte-Marie-du-Mont.

FIERCE LOCAL BATTLES

Swiftly rallied by their officers and NCOs, the disparate groups of intermingled American paratroopers quickly formed ad hoc task forces and set off on foot to seize their objectives. A conglomeration of 630 troops from the 502nd PIR (which were intended to arrive at DZ-A) managed to form into cohesive units; these struck east to seize the key road junctions around Saint-Martin-de-Varreville, as well as the Utah Beach Exits 3 and 4, located further east. Other mixed elements that had reached DZ-C and DZ-D simultaneously fought their way east to seize Beach Exits 1 and 2.

Throughout much of D-Day, fierce local battles unfolded between the dozen separated groupings of 101st Division assets and local German garrisons. These confused actions certainly disrupted German attempts to mount counter-attacks against the forces landing on Utah Beach.

Moreover, during the afternoon and evening of 6 June, several US infantry battalions that had landed at Utah successfully fought their way westwards to link up with the most easterly pockets of paratroopers, those located around Saint-Martin-de-Varreville and Audouville-la-Hubert.

82ND AIRBORNE DROP ZONES

The formation of transport planes that was carrying the soldiers of the US 82nd Airborne Division had, as mentioned before, crossed the Cotentin's western coastline around Barneville-Carteret heading on a bearing of east-southeast. Continuing on that route, the aircraft began dropping in height as they crossed the base of the Cotentin Peninsula. Here, they encountered dense clouds, as well as heavy fire from enemy flak guns. The required evasive manoeuvres caused the "Vic-of-Vic" formations to break apart.

Soon, the aircraft were approaching the three Divisional Drop-Zones, two of which lay west of the inundated Merderet valley and one to the west. These locations were: DZ-N, to the north of Picauville, which lay west of the flooded north-to-south axis of the Merderet valley; DZ-T, located north-northeast of DZ-N, also to the west of the Merderet; and finally, DZ-O, located east of the Merderet valley to the northwest of the important road junction at Sainte-Mère-Église.

GLIDER TOWING

During last light on 5 June 1944, three American C-47 transport aircraft each tow a Waco CG-4A glider out across the Channel, passing over Allied vessels heading south.

FLOODED MEADOWS

Within but a few seconds of the aerial formations beginning to break up – around 0430 hrs – the transport aircraft pilots then either had to release glider tow ropes or signal the 10-man para sticks to start jumping, while still taking violent evasive action to escape the bursts of German anti-aircraft fire. As with the 101st, the 82nd Division's landings were horribly scattered with many units intermingled with others. Just a few sticks successfully landed west of the Merderet, on DZ-N and DZ-T; most of their compatriots landed further east, in the middle of the flooded Merderet water meadows. There was a better grouping of forces at DZ-O, albeit including sticks slated for the other two DZs; indeed, few of the 52 gliders due to land at DZ-O did so.

WACO GLIDER
Crashing on landing, this Waco
CG-4A glider has flipped over
with its front staved-in; eight
of the glider's complement
have perished, their bodies
respectfully laid out on the
ground with faces covered.

In total, 277 American troops died during the drop, most to drowning. Once again, company and platoon commanders swiftly scooped up whatever force they could that was east of the valley and marched off towards Sainte-Mère-Église. To the west of the valley, officers similarly grabbed various elements and marched them eastwards to seize the two key bridges over the Merderet near Amfreville and Chef-du-Pont, and the nearby bridge over the Douve at Pont l'Abbé.

DEFENCE AT SAINTE-MÈRE-ÉGLISE

During the afternoon of 6 June, the three pockets of isolated soldiers from the US 82nd Airborne Division located west of the River Merderet faced repeated small local enemy incursions. Most of these attacks were mounted by newly arriving elements of the German 91st

ABOVE:
BOMBING MISSION
In the early morning of D-Day, having completed its mission, a Ninth US Army Air Force Martin B-26 Marauder bomber flies back north to England, passing over dozens of Allied vessels steaming south.

OPPOSITE ABOVE:
82ND AIRBORNE DIVISION
Soldiers from the 82nd Airborne Division check their equipment before the first airborne assault on the continent, 5 June 1944. A Horsa glider, painted with invasion stripes, is visible in the background.

OPPOSITE BELOW:
SAINTE-MÈRE-ÉGLISE
Rienforcements of the Third US Army march past the church of Sainte-Mère-Église, July 1944. On the night of 5/6 June, a well-known incident involved paratrooper John Steele of the 505th Parachute Infantry Regiment (PIR), whose parachute caught on the spire of the town church. He hung there for two hours, before the Germans took him prisoner. Steele later escaped when paratroopers of the 3rd Battalion 505 PIR attacked and captured the village.

TAKING A BREATHER
Paratroopers of the 82nd
Airborne Division relaxing after
liberating the village of Sainte-
Mère-Église, 8 June 1944. The
shoulder patch of the nearest
standing soldier has been erased,
presumably by the censors.

Infantry Division. By midnight, these German ripostes had managed either to partially overrun these American positions or force the troops to exfiltrate in small groups. Only a few of these parties successfully managed to get across the river and attach themselves to the paratrooper-held enclaves to the east.

One still-cohesive small American force, however, did manage to hold the positions they had established close to the Chef-du-Pont Bridge, denying its use to the enemy. Further to the east, meanwhile, some 1,200 troops of the 505th PIR had managed to successfully seize the key transportation node at Sainte-Mère-Église. Here, they established a firm defensive perimeter around the village, significantly hampering the movements of German reserves heading south and southeast in attempts to contain the amphibious landings on Utah Beach.

AD HOC ENGAGEMENTS

The accuracy of the insertion of the 13,000 troops of the US 82nd and 101st Airborne Divisions delivered early on D-Day was significantly worse than Allied planners had, perhaps somewhat naively, anticipated. The forces inserted into the theatre were significantly scattered and intermingled. Through the initiative and courage of junior leaders, ad hoc task forces nonetheless endeavoured to secure their objectives.

ARMING UP A TYPHOON
Ground crew arm an RAF Hawker Typhoon ground-attack aircraft. The Typhoon was equipped with eight RP-3 unguided air-to-ground rockets, each with a 27kg (60lb) warhead. Twenty-six squadrons of Typhoon were deployed on 6 June1944, and in the coming weeks destroyed hundreds of German armoured fighting vehicles to aid the ground advance.

While over half of these were not achieved, the American airborne landings nevertheless achieved their task of disrupting the German response to the Allied landings on Utah Beach. In particular, the 82nd Division's seizure of the key road junction at Sainte-Mère-Église significantly hindered the movement of German reserves.

Furthermore, even when paratrooper units failed to secure an objective, the many local engagements in which they got embroiled fixed in contact many small German units that could have instead struck east to block the egress through the marshland causeways

of the US forces landed on Utah Beach. Sadly, the courageous American paratroopers paid a heavy price for these achievements on 6 June: they suffered some 2,499 casualties – a staggering 19 per cent of the force that had left the UK just a few hours previously.

BRITISH 6TH AIRBORNE DIVISION

As this bitter airborne fighting played out across the invasion's western flank, a similar story unfolded in the east, beyond the River Orne. The Overlord assault plan had envisaged that during the early hours of 6 June, prior to the beach landings, some 11,000 troops

OPPOSITE:
101ST AIRBORNE DIVISION
Resolute faces of US paratroopers just before they took off for the initial assault of D-Day. The paratrooper in the foreground had just read General Dwight D. Eisenhower's message of good luck and clasped his bazooka in determination. Note Eisenhower's D-Day order in the hands of the paratrooper in the foreground.

ABOVE:
LANDING NEAR THE ORNE RIVER
Three large British Hamilcar gliders from the British 6th Airborne Division's second landing wave about to land in a open crop field located east of the River Orne, 6 June 1944.

from Major-General Gale's British 6th Airborne Division would be inserted into the area east of the Orne. The Division's main objectives were to seize or destroy seven bridges over the key water obstacles that intersected this low-lying area, which the Germans had deliberately inundated to impede any enemy advance through it.

The 6th Airborne Division's objectives included capturing the bridges over the Caen Canal at Bénouville and over the River Orne just to the east. Holding these bridges would prevent the Germans from destroying them, thus hindering any enemy attempt to retard any eastward Allied exploitation from Sword Beach. Other elements of the division were to destroy three bridges further east over the River Dives. The destruction of these bridges would slow or disrupt the westward movement of German armoured reserves to counter-attack the vulnerable Sword beachhead from the east and southeast during those critical hours of D-Day.

GLIDER INSERTION

During 2245–2255 hrs on 5 June, three RAF Halifax bombers took off from RAF Tarrant Rushton in Dorset towing three Horsa gliders slated for the assault on the "Pegasus" Bridge spanning the Caen Canal at Bénouville, adjacent to the Orne. Thereafter, three more Halifax-towed gliders carried the troops slated to seize the nearby River Orne Bridge. Led by Major John Howard, the "Pegasus" taskforce consisted of 91 men from the 2nd Ox and Bucks Light Infantry and a Royal Engineers unit. Having travelled across the Channel, between 0015 and 0019 hrs on 6 June the bombers released the three Horsa gliders, which glided down to land near the bridge.

FINAL BRIEFING
A platoon of Pathfinders from the 22nd Independent Parachute Company, British 6th Airborne Division, receive a final briefing on their D-Day mission during the afternoon of 5 June 1944.

The crossing at Bénouville was defended by two platoons from the 642nd East Battalion, attached to the 716th (Static) Infantry Division. This unit had German officers and NCOs but its rank-and-file were former Soviet Army soldiers captured by the Germans in the East; these men had reluctantly "volunteered" to fight for the Germans to avoid death through privation and disease in appalling prisoner-of-war labour camps. Their limited combat motivation was revealed on D-Day by their lethargic responses to the initial British attack on the bridge.

"PEGASUS" BRIDGE ASSAULT

At 0016 hrs, the glider transporting Major Howard, Lt Brotheridge's 23-man platoon and five sappers landed first, coming to a juddering stop 47m (51 yards) short of the bridge's eastern end. The complacent German sentries, assuming this was an Allied aircraft crashing, did not even investigate. Next, at 0017 hrs, the second glider carrying Lt Wood's platoon landed relatively smoothly, but 500m (547 yards) south-southeast of the bridge. By then, Brotheridge's men were racing towards the bridge, firing weapons from the hip. Led by Brotheridge, 10 soldiers dashed across the bridge, still firing from the hip. The now alert German troops on the canal's western bank returned fire, fatally wounding Brotheridge.

Meanwhile, another paratrooper section had overwhelmed enemy resistance in the two dugouts located near the bridge's southeastern corner. Next, five sappers rushed across the

FIELD OF GLIDERS
This oblique aerial view depicts 12 Horsa gliders, plus some laid-out parachutes from the 6th Airborne Division at Landing Zone "N" near Ranville, 6 June 1944.

bridge and negated the enemy's preparations to destroy the bridge. Finally, at 0018 hrs, the third glider landed violently in between the other two and promptly sank into the marshy pond.

The surviving troops quickly moved across the bridge and reinforced the battle to secure its western approaches. By 0022 hrs, Howard's men had secured the entire position and they then expanded their defensive perimeter westwards into the eastern fringes of Bénouville. In just six minutes, the Allies had liberated the first part of German-occupied France.

DEFENDING THE BRIDGE

Subsequently, Howard's troops consolidated their defensive positions around the bridge and in Bénouville village. They were reinforced when 195 troops from the 6th Airborne Division's 7th Parachute Regiment arrived around 0230 hrs. Over the next 12 hours, Howard's men held doggedly, despite facing repeated local counter-attacks mounted by elements of the 21st Panzer Division. These ripostes typically involved a platoon or two of dismounted enemy panzergrenadiers, supported by a couple of AFVs, either Panzer IV tanks or Marder I self-propelled anti-tank vehicles. In addition, around 0900 hrs, two small enemy gunboats, which had moved south down the canal from Ouistreham, engaged Howard's dug-in soldiers at the bridge. Fierce fire from several paratrooper PIAT anti-tank teams, however, forced both vehicles to withdraw.

In the meantime, the Allied units that had landed on Sword Beach that morning were striving to advance southeast to link up with Howard's men. At 1335 hrs on D-Day, the spearheads of the British 1st Special Service (Commando) Brigade, subordinated to 3rd

"PEGASUS" BRIDGE
Taken several days after D-Day, this view from "Pegasus" Bridge's western end shows Allied traffic passing across it; note how close the nearest glider has landed to the bridge.

Infantry Division on D-Day, arrived at Bénouville. They swiftly relieved Howard's exhausted men of the critical task of continuing to deny the bridge to counter-attacking German forces.

MERVILLE BATTERY

Another key 6th Airborne Division mission was that to neutralize the four potent German 15.5cm (6.1in) artillery pieces located at Merville Battery, 4.3km (2.7 miles) southeast of Sword Beach on the eastern side of the Orne estuary. The Allies believed that these guns posed a serious threat to the success of the landings on Sword Beach. One of the 6th Division's battalions – the 9th Battalion, the Parachute Regiment ("9 Para") – was thus tasked with temporarily neutralizing the guns over the period of the initial landings, rather than seizing the battery or destroying the guns.

During spring 1944, 9 Para's commander, Lt-Col Terence Otway, developed a complex plan for the battalion's assault on Merville, timed for 0430 hrs on 6 June. As his paratrooper-rifle platoons mounted their assault from the wooden blocks located east of the battery, three Horsa gliders would stage a simultaneous surprise *coup de main* air assault inside the battery perimeter. The gliders carried additional paratroopers but also engineer troops with specialized demolition equipment to neutralize the guns.

During 0050–0130 hrs on 6 June, the 750-strong 9 Para dropped in the area east of Gonneville-en-Auge but west of Varaville. With the transport planes forced into violent evasive manoeuvres by heavy flak bursts, the timed dropping of

GLIDER TROOPS

Three of the British glider-delivered airborne troops who landed at "Pegasus" Bridge; the one on the left casually rests his section's bipod-fitted 7.69mm (0.303in) Bren light machine gun over his left shoulder. The officer in the centre carries a Sten gun with bayonet fixed.

the 10-person paratrooper sticks was significantly disrupted. Consequently, 9 Para's soldiers landed badly dispersed with some troops landing 3.5km (2.2 miles) northeast of the DZ. The assembled entire battalion was supposed to depart the DZ Rendezvous Point – located some 1.8km (1.1 miles) southeast of the battery – at 0240 hrs. By then, however, only 150 out of 750 paras had managed to assemble. Despite this, these 150 troops silently marched northwestwards through the darkness along tracks and secondary roads.

Passing through Gonneville undetected, due in part to no dogs barking, 9 Para's remnants eventually formed up in a wood just east of the battery's eastern perimeter fence. In the meantime, a recce party had infiltrated up to the battery's inner wire and had ascertained that the aerial strike by 102 Lancaster bombers at 0040 hrs had neither breached the wire nor inflicted much damage on the battery.

At 0430 hrs, 9 Para's remnants assaulted the battery, although none of the three *coup de main* gliders managed to land within its perimeter. The paratroopers breached the battery's eastern perimeter wire and then charged through the gaps, guns blazing, while a diversionary group assaulted the battery's northern (main) gate. The paras assaulting from the east, reinforced by the diversion group that had fought its way through the main gate, were soon locked into bitter, confused, hand-to-hand combat with the battery's defenders.

By 0500 hrs, the paras had secured much of the battery. Lacking the demolition assets carried in the three missing gliders, the paras swifty disabled the guns using improvised methods (such as throwing away a breach block or destroying the elevation mechanism). The assault, however, had incurred painful losses, with 25 paratroopers killed and 42 wounded. Ironically, the troops discovered that the four enemy guns were actually ex-Czech 10cm (3.9in) field guns, not the deadlier 15.5cm (6.1in) pieces forecasted by Allied intelligence. With a planned Allied naval bombardment of the battery imminent, Otway's combat-shocked men swiftly withdrew.

RIVER DIVES BRIDGES

Meanwhile, the 6th Airborne Division's remaining units were striving to achieve other additional missions early on 6 June. Its battalions were to destroy four bridges over the southward course of the River Dives. These targets included the road ridge at Saint-Clair, near Robehomme, the road and rail bridges at Bures, and the road bridge at Troarn. Other 6th Airborne units were also to destroy the bridge over the River Divette at Varaville. Further objectives included capturing all of the key high ground of the Bois de Bavent and the Bois de Bures. Despite experiencing significant dispersal on landing, the 6th Division's troops managed to achieve most of these objectives, including the destruction of the bridges. These operations succeeded in disrupting the German counter-attacks being launched westwards towards the River Orne from the areas east of the Dives.

This achievement, secured with 630 troop casualties, provided the protection required for the landings on Sword Beach to firmly consolidate the beachhead and subsequently advance inland to the south and southeast. By midnight, these exploitation forces had linked up with some of the 6th Division's units.

CROSSROADS
On 7 June 1944, outside Ranville, two paratroopers from the British 6th Airborne Division scan the road ahead for signs of enemy troops; the one in the foreground wields a 9mm (0.35in) Sten Mark V submachine gun.

LINK-UP
With smiles of relief, on 9 June, 12 Para soldiers, who had landed several miles away from their intended drop-zone and spent three days evading the enemy, finally link up with their comrades.

SUPPORT FROM THE BEACH
Sherman DD tanks of "B" Squadron, 13th/18th Royal Hussars support men of No. 4 Commando, 1st Special Service Brigade, on the Rue de Riva-Bella in Ouistreham, 6 June 1944. Lord Lovat's 1st Special Service Brigade from Sword Beach had reached "Pegasus" Bridge by the afternoon of 6 June 1944.

B-26 MARAUDERS
View of a squadron of USAAF Martin B-26 Marauder medium bombers, taken by one of the crews' flying in this formation, heading toward the Normandy coast during June 1944; they sport the black-and-white 'Invasion' recognition scheme applied to most aircraft during 3–4 June 1944.

ABOVE:
MOSQUITO FIGHTER-BOMBER
This de Havilland Mosquito twin-engined fighter-bomber has been fitted out in the Overlord aerial-recognition camouflage scheme, which comprised five bands of alternating white and black colour (three white, two black) applied around the aircraft's wings and fuselage.

RIGHT:
FLY BOYS
American fighter pilots plan the route for their next mission over Normandy, using the wing of one of their Republic P-47 Thunderbolt fighters; this capable aircraft design flew no fewer than 746,000 sorties during World War II.

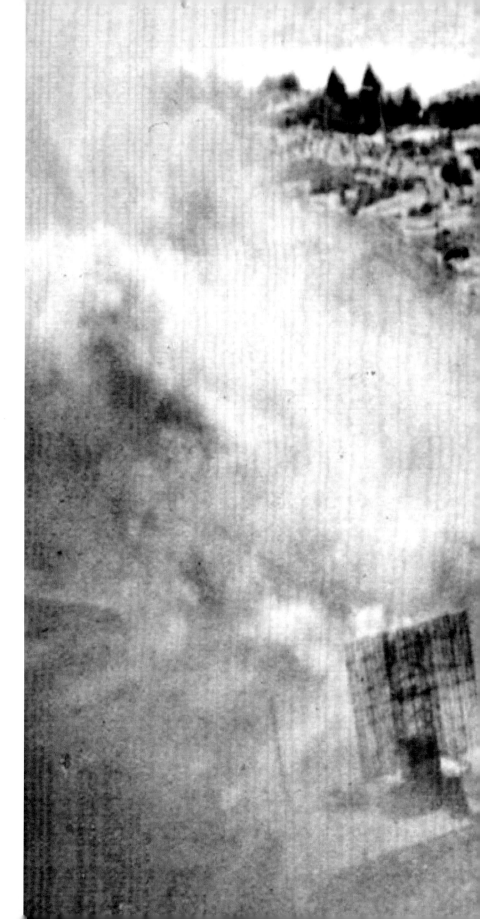

THE AMERICAN BEACHES

Along the western flank of the Normandy invasion sector, the American amphibious assaults on Utah and Omaha beaches commenced at 0630 hrs. The preliminary naval bombardments by Bombardment Groups "U" and "O" had commenced at 0550 hrs, with the Western Task Force's allocated LCT-Rs adding their weight of fire at 0620 hrs. The spearhead forces of General Collins' VII US Corps were to assault Utah Beach, while the vanguard of General Leonard Gerow's US V Corps attacked Omaha. By midnight on 6 June, Collins' forces at Omaha were supposed to have successfully established a beachhead across the southeastern corner of the Cotentin Peninsula. This was intended to stretch north to south from Quinéville down to Carentan, as well as to have secured an inland advance of up to 16km (10 miles) to reach the River Douve at Pont l'Abbé. Simultaneously, Gerow's forces were tasked with establishing a 23km (14 mile)-wide beachhead, with a maximum depth of 8km (5 miles); in the east of this beachhead, Gerow's forces were slated to have linked up with the westward advance of the British forces landed at Gold Beach.

OPPOSITE:
SHIP-TO-SHIP
American troops disembark from a large landing vessel, possibly a Landing Craft, Infantry (Large) – or LCI(L) for short – to a much-smaller LCVP to be transported to the shoreline of the Normandy coast.

EN ROUTE
American infantrymen crowd
into a US Navy Landing Craft,
Infantry (LCI) during D-Day,
prior to being transferred to
different landing craft for the
beach assault.

UTAH BEACH

Utah Beach, the most westerly Allied landing zone, ran along the Cotentin Peninsula's southeastern coast. Utah lay 21km (13 miles) west of Omaha, with both beaches separated by a major geographical obstacle: the Baie des Veys, an extensive coastal inlet, into which the marshy estuaries of the rivers Vire and Douve emptied.

Along Utah, three battalions from the 709th (static) Infantry Division manned the 10 coastal strongpoints that stretched from Les Dunes de Varreville in the north down to Pouppeville. Behind this were deployed the artillery batteries at Azeville, Saint-Marcouf and Saint-Martin-de-Varreville.

Compared to the other invasion beaches, Utah was covered by relatively modest enemy defences. This was partly because the Germans believed that their deliberate inundation of the low-lying hinterland behind the initial strip of beach dunes provided the area with a strong natural defence. Any westward Allied advance inland would be canalized on to just the four narrow causeways that stretched across the flooded marshy strip, which had a maximum width of 5km (3 miles). Running from north to south, the Allies termed these causeways Exits 1, 2, 3 and 4.

STRONGPOINT WN-05

Strongpoint WN-05 was typical of the 10 Resistance Nests the German forces had constructed along the coast sector the Allies termed "Utah". WN-05 was located at La Madeleine Plage, and covered the narrow road – Exit 2 – that crossed the marshy hinterland to Sainte-Marie-du-Mont. WN-05 was of a squat rectangular arrangement, with its long

LCVP
Men on board a Coast Guard manned Landing Craft, Infantry LCI(L) attend Mass while en route to the invasion beaches, June 1944.

(broadly north to south) axis facing the sea and the west-to-east-running road bisecting it laterally through the centre. The site was 370m (405 yards) long and 275m (301 yards) deep. The beach was 800m (875 yards) wide at low tide, but at high tide the water came right up to the narrow strip of shallow dunes, along which the Germans had laid barbed wire. The strongpoint fielded various weapons: a 7.5cm (2.95in) FK 38 field gun; two 5cm (1.97in) KwK L/50 ex-tank guns; an ex-French 4.7cm (1.85in) PaK 181(f) anti-tank gun; two tripod-mounted MG42 heavy machine guns; an ex-French 7.5mm (2.95in) MG311 Reibel armoured-car gun; a captured 8.14cm GrWr 278(f) heavy mortar; as well as two flame-throwers and five Goliath demolition tankettes. The position was defended by a platoon, plus an attached fourth section, from the 3rd Company of the 709th Division's 919th Grenadier Regiment.

INVASION FLEET SIGHTED

As darkness lifted, binocular-using German sentries at WN-05 spotted hundreds of tiny blobs emerging over the horizon; moving steadily towards them, the observers soon identified them as enemy vessels. Within 30 minutes, a vast Allied fleet was visible to WN-05's defenders: off Utah Beach were now positioned the 865 vessels of Task Force 125, commanded by American Rear Admiral Don Moon from the attack transport USS *Bayfield* (APA-33).

Moon's command was half of American Rear Admiral Alan Kirk's Western Task Force. A key element of Moon's armada were the 20 warships of Bombardment Group "U". This comprised 13 American ships, six Royal Navy vessels and one Dutch gunboat.

TRANSFER LCVP TO LCIL

American troops transfer from an LCVP to the Landing Craft, Infantry (Large) USS 539, while loading for the invasion; when fully loaded with 188 troops, this LCI(I) displaced 395 tonnes (389 tons).

The group's most potent assets were the American battleship USS *Nevada* (BB-36), mounting ten 35.5cm (14in) guns, and the British Monitor HMS *Erebus*, with her two 38.1cm (15in) guns. Supporting them were three American heavy cruisers and two RN light cruisers – HMS *Black Prince,* sporting eight 133mm (5.25in) guns, and HMS *Enterprise*, with its seven 152mm (6in) barrels. These warships protected the 785 transport vessels slated to operate at Utah, which included seven LSI(L)s, 34 LCTs, 16 Landing Craft, Mechanised (LCMs), and 389 LCVPs.

ASSAULT PLAN

The American plan envisaged that the US 8th and 12th Regimental Combat Teams (RCTs), supported by two tank battalions, would assault sectors Tare (Green) and Uncle (Red); the 22nd RCT would then follow up. Once an initial beachhead had been established, the five 12th and 22nd RCT battalions landed that morning would advance in three directions: north-northwest along the coast to Quinéville; west through the marshes along Exit 4 and then north-northwest to Crisbecq; and west through the marshes via Exit 4 and then northwest to Écausseville.

Simultaneously, the 8th RCT's three battalions would advance southwest and south through the marshes via Exits 1 and 2 to Sainte-Marie-du-Mont, Hiesville and Les Forges to link up with the 82nd and 101st Airborne Division units that had been dropped behind enemy lines. After accurate naval and aerial bombardments during 0550–0629 hrs, the first infantry waves disembarked from their LCVPs at 0630 hrs. Driven off-course by the pounding waves, these troops landed 900m (984 yards) further south than planned, on Uncle (Red) and Victor sectors.

Stunned by the preliminary bombardments, the defenders offered less intense resistance than they did elsewhere. Indeed, within just 60 minutes, the

RANGER TRAINING
During May 1944, US Army Rangers undertake training for the planned assault on the Pointe du Hoc promontory, practising drills connected to the use of long extendable scaling ladders to climb its cliffs.

assaulting American forces had managed to overrun three German strongpoints and had established a small beachhead.

ALLIED LOSSES AT UTAH

At Utah during the late morning and afternoon, the 4th US Division's spearheads continued determinedly to push inland. They faced stiffening, but still relatively modest, enemy resistance as reinforcements from the German 91st Infantry Division gradually arrived. The 4th Division's units managed to advance northwest towards the Azeville Battery, while other units drove west to close in on the American airborne forces that had seized Sainte-Mère-Église. Simultaneously, two battalions pushed southwest towards Sainte-Marie-du-Mont.

The unfolding Allied advance continued until the last embers of daylight had passed. Indeed, by midnight, the 4th Division had secured a large beachhead that stretched for 16km (10 miles) north to south out to a maximum depth of 13km (8 miles). Its forces had reached Hameau des Cruttes on the coast, closed in on Ravenoville in the north, approached Sainte-Mère-Église and Les Forges in the west, and cleared Sainte-Marie-du-Mont in the south. Its forces had also linked up with American airborne units in the areas east of Sainte-Mère-Église and southwest of Sainte-Marie-du-Mont.

POINTE DU HOC

The Allies had landed 19,500 troops on to Utah Beach during D-Day and these forces had incurred 296 casualties; however, the US airborne forces

dropped that day behind Utah Beach had paid the dreadful price of 2,499 casualties suffered. Between Utah and Omaha beaches, 5km (2 miles) west of Omaha, there was a lesser-known Allied landing site, the Pointe du Hoc promontory. American forces were tasked with neutralizing the German artillery battery perched on the top of the rocky outcrop's 35m (110ft)-tall cliffs.

The strongpoint was manned by the 2nd Battery, Army Coastal Artillery Battalion 1260 and a 352nd Division infantry platoon. The battery housed six ex-French 1917-vintage 15.5cm (6.1in) GPF K418(f) artillery pieces.

SCALING THE CLIFFS

At 0710 hrs, some 235 2nd and 5th US Ranger Battalion troops – half the force slated for the task – successfully landed at the base of the cliffs. Using mortar-delivered grappling hooks and tall ladders, the Rangers scrambled up the cliffs; in some cases, the alerted defenders pushed the ladders away, toppling the Rangers into the rocky waters below. The attackers encountered fierce enemy resistance but nonetheless managed to fight their way deep into the battery and repel two enemy ripostes.

Unfortunately, after incurring 77 fatalities and many wounded, they found the six bunkers empty; the Germans had recently moved the 15.5cm (6.1in) guns inland. Two patrols headed inland, however, and managed to neutralize most of the guns.

ARTILLERY BUNKERS
German prisoners-of-war are marched past the remnants of the concrete bunkers of Pointe du Hoc. The precipitous position of the defences is obvious from this photograph.

AFTER THE ASSAULT
Having stormed the cliffs at
Pointe du Hoc and cleared
the enemy position, these
exhausted US Rangers grab
some well-earned rest, to take
on water and eat some rations
(from the Navy Collection, US
National Archives).

TROOPS RACE ACROSS UTAH BEACH
After disembarking from their landing craft and wading ashore, American infantry charge across the exposed killing zone of the flat sands on Utah Beach, on the morning of D-Day.

OPPOSITE:
AERIAL VIEW OF UTAH BEACH
A fascinating aerial view of the US 4th Infantry Division's assault on Utah Beach unfolding; visible are four large landing craft offshore, three assault craft and a column of four vehicles moving through the shallows.

RIGHT:
MEDICAL AID
Three US Army medics attend to a wounded soldier on Utah Beach during D-Day; the medic on the right is taking the soldier's pulse with his right hand while holding a pair of surgical scissors in his left.

BELOW:
SEA WALL
Soldiers from the US 4th Division's 8th Infantry Regiment move out over the concrete sea wall on Utah Beach; some of their comrades take a rest behind the wall.

LEFT:
TROOPS LAND
A platoon of heavily laden American infantry wade through the shallows on to the sand on Utah Beach during the afternoon of D-Day; behind them it seems that an Allied vehicle is disembarking through the double doors of a beached LCT.

BELOW:
TAKING SHELTER
American infantry rest their weary bodies, sitting back against a low concrete wall at Utah Beach; their comrade in the centre appears to be re-sorting his personal kit and equipment.

ABOVE:
WADING ASHORE
A platoon from the US 4th Infantry Division wade through the thigh-deep surf towards Utah Beach (in the background); several of them are attempting to keep their rifles well clear of the water.

LEFT:
VIEW FROM AN LST
A US Army vehicle moves through the shallows towards Utah Beach; the vehicle's Browning 12.7mm (0.5in) M2-HB heavy machine gun points skywards for anti-aircraft defence (from the Army Signal Corps Collection).

INCOMING ARTILLERY
A large explosion occurs on
Utah Beach, probably caused
by a German artillery round,
on the morning of 6 June 1944;
in the foreground, US soldiers
take cover to protect themselves
from enemy fire.

OMAHA BEACH

Omaha, the eastern American beach, lay 14.5km (9 miles) west of the right (western) flank of the most westerly of the Anglo-Canadian beaches – Gold. The 1st US Infantry Division, the spearhead of General Gerow's
US V Corps, was slated to assault Omaha.
The division's assault sector extended for 8km (4 miles) west to east from Vierville through to Sainte-Honorine-des-Pertes. The terrain on Omaha was particularly challenging, with steep bluffs situated immediately behind the top of the beach. Through these bluffs there merely ran four V-profile draws, termed D-1 (at Vierville), D-3 (Saint-Laurent), E-1 (northeast of Saint-Laurent) and E-3 (Colleville-sur-Mer). This restrictive terrain channelled any attempted Allied advance inland into these draws, which were heavily defended.

To soften up the German defences before the assault, between 0556 and 0610 hrs some 624 American B-24 bombers attacked enemy positions. Unfortunately, due to the bad weather, and anti-fratricide aiming delays, many of the 13,100 bombs fell behind the German coastal defences. Meanwhile, at 0550 hrs, the preliminary naval warship bombardment had begun, with 37 artillery guns and 34 tanks on LCTs joining in at 0602 hrs. Regrettably, poor visibility and the heavily pitching waters hampered the accuracy of the naval fire support.

On 6 June, the German defensive positions along Omaha Beach were manned by troops from the German 352nd (field) Infantry Division. This formation had only arrived in the area in May 1944,

FINAL APPROACH
American infantry, some with mesh-netted helmets, approach Omaha Beach on D-Day; in front of them on the beach are numerous vehicles; the smoke generated by the explosions caused by enemy artillery rounds can also be seen.

ABOVE TOP:
LCVP
The LCVP designated PA13-22, from the troopship APA-13
USS *Joseph T. Dickman*, a converted cruise ship, transports troops,
some of whom wear life vests; in the background, a Rhino ferry
carries ambulances.

ABOVE LOWER:
TRUCK LOAD
An assortment of American soft-skinned vehicles, three of which
sport national insignia aerial-recognition devices on their roofs, have
been loaded on to a landing craft that is heading for Utah Beach.

OPPOSITE:
GERMAN MACHINE-GUN NEST
A German fire-support team man a tripod-mounted, heavy-role
MG34 machine gun from within what appears to be a small,
low-set, pillbox-style emplacement; note the two stick grenades
positioned to the right of the weapon.

taking over coastal sectors previously held by the 716th (static) Division. Alas, in a rare intelligence failing, the Allies had not detected this development. The greater than expected enemy troop densities, less successful than anticipated preliminary bombardments, and difficult terrain made successfully assaulting Omaha particularly challenging. The western half of Omaha – from Vierville through to Colleville – was defended by the 916th Grenadier Regiment (plus attached units from the 716th Division's 726th Grenadier Regiment) and fell within Coastal Defence Sector II.

The eastern flank of Omaha Beach, from Colleville eastwards to Sainte-Honorine, fell within the Coastal Defence Sector III; it was defended by the 726th Regiment's I and II Battalions. These units manned 11 Resistance Nests along Omaha Beach, running from WN-72 in the west through to WN-60 in the east. In addition, the 22 guns from the 352nd

Division's artillery regiment, deployed up to 3.2km (2 miles) behind the coast, supported these coastal strongpoints.

GERMAN STRONGPOINTS

WN-62 was typical of the 11 strongpoints the Germans had constructed along the coastline the Allies designated Omaha Beach. WN-62 was manned by a 31-strong platoon from the 3rd Company, I Battalion, 726th Grenadier Regiment, one of the 716th Division's units attached to the 352nd Division. It was positioned along the northwest entrance to the E-3 Draw at Colleville-sur-Mer near the hamlet of Les Moulins, opposite the Fox (Green) Sector. WN-62 fielded four principal weapons: a 7.5cm (2.95in) Pak 40 anti-tank gun; two pre-1914 7.5cm (2.95in) FK235(b) field guns captured from the Belgians in 1940; and a 5cm (1.97in) KwK L/50 ex-tank gun. In addition, WN-62 sported two tripod-mounted MG42s,

a 5cm (1.97in) mortar, and two flame-throwers. It possessed five principal installations: one Vf69 bunker, a Vf61a bunker, two R669 casemates and an unfinished R667 casemate.

It was against these 11 German Resistance Nests along Omaha that the full fury of the Allied onslaught would fall. First, there would come preliminary bombardments by dozens of warships and hundreds of medium bombers, followed by many hundreds of assault troops and dozens of AFVs disembarking on to the beach in front of the dazed and shocked defenders.

VAST ARMADA

Indeed, in the dawn half-light, the on-duty observer at WN-62 reported spotting hundreds of enemy vessels approaching them, with many more in the distance stretching as far as his binoculars could see. Bewildered, the sentry shouted, "That's not possible, there's not that many ships in the entire world!" Yet a "mere" 1,028 vessels from the 6,939-strong Allied maritime armada had been allocated to operate off Omaha. These vessels hailed from American Rear Admiral John Hall's Task Force "O".

This command was sub-divided into four sub-elements: the bombardment group; the assault group; the assault support echelon; and the mine-sweeping force. The 19 vessels of the bombardment group comprised two American battleships (USS *Arkansas* and USS *Texas*), two RN and two French light cruisers, 10 US Navy destroyers and two RN escort destroyers.

RIGHT:
RHINO FERRIES
Often operated by crews of SeaBees – US Naval Construction Battalion personnel – these Rhino ferries were typically employed during D-Day to transfer vehicles from large vessels sitting offshore right up to the shoreline.

OVERLEAF:
LCVP
A small landing craft transports a platoon of US 1st Division assault infantry troops towards Omaha Beach; note that several of the soldiers have covered their rifles with waterproofed material.

The assault force, which would deliver the ground forces on to the beach, included eight American Attack Transports, four British LSI(L)s, six LSI(Small)s, 14 LSTs, 84 LCTs, 13 LCMs and 386 LCVPs. The 67 vessels of the assault support group, which provided fire support to the assaulting forces, included 14 LCT-Rs and six LCFs. Finally, the anti-mine element consisted of 41 British and Canadian mine-sweepers.

DD SHERMANS FAIL TO LAND

The Allied assault unfolded across nine sectors, with Dog, Easy and Fox running from west to east, sub-divided into (Green), (White) and (Red). At 0615 hrs, two RCTs, supported by two tank battalions and

BEACH OBSTACLES
At Omaha, the American first-wave infantry wading towards shore met withering enemy machine-gun fire that killed or wounded many of them; the shocked survivors went to ground, desperately seeking shelter behind enemy beach obstacles.

four Ranger companies, initiated the assault. Across Dog, the 116th RCT (attached from 29th Division) landed, while across Easy and Fox sectors the 16th RCT assaulted. At 0545 hrs, LSTs carrying the 122 first-wave Shermans disgorged the 29 lead amphibious DD Shermans into the deeply swelling waters some 4.8km (3 miles) offshore; sadly, 27 of them sank.

The remaining LSTs instead steamed inshore and delivered the remaining DD Shermans on to the beach at around 0614 hrs. Next, at 0615 hrs, the first wave of infantry disembarked from LCAs and LCVPs into neck-deep, swirling waters; they were often far from their intended landing spots. As the infantry waded ashore, they faced a hail of German machine-gun fire,

which swiftly inflicted many casualties. When the lead survivors reached the gently rising beach, they faced (at half tide) a 150m (492ft)-wide strip of sand and shingle.

As the bedraggled infantry tried to advance up the beach they were mown down by intense, accurate German fire; some of the gravely wounded were subsequently drowned by the incoming tide.

The next tranche of American infantry reached the beach at 0621 hrs, only to be similarly cut down by withering enemy fire. By now, all the soldiers on the beach had gone to ground, seeking shelter behind beach obstacles or shallow sand-scrapes while courageously struggling to return fire.

LEFT:
LAND CRAFT APPROACH
A variety of Allied landing craft
– including a LCVP in the right
foreground – move towards
Omaha Beach on the morning
of 6 June 1944.

BELOW:
LCT US 207 LANDS
At 1600 hrs on D-Day, the
American Mark 5 LCT
designated USS 207 has
just beached itself at Dog
(Red) Sector on Omaha; it is
transporting the 58th Armored
Field Battalion's self-propelled
artillery pieces.

ABOVE:
RAMP DOWN
In this iconic D-Day image, taken from the back of an LCVP, a platoon of heavily laden American infantry wade through waist-high water to approach the exposed, smoke-filled expanse of Omaha Beach.

LEFT:
CASUALTIES
The corpses of four American assault troops from the 1st US Division's 16th RCT who perished during the assault on Omaha have been laid out in a row close to the waterline, opposite Colleville-sur-Mer.

Over the next 40 minutes, the troops of each RCT's reserve battalion landed on Omaha and met the same intense resistance. By then, only seven platoon-sized groupings had made it across the beach to the relative shelter of the sea wall or the bottom of the bluffs.

Inspired by nearby leader-figures, these few groups began, using fire-and-movement, to work their way inland up the bluffs. Indeed, by 0735 hrs, some American troops had managed to fight themselves inland to attack the flanks of strongpoints WN-61 and WN-62, opposite Fox (Green). Next, at 0750 hrs, US Brigadier-General Norman Cota coordinated disparate stragglers to breach the wire on Dog (Green), just east of Les Moulins between WN-68 and WN-70, and led these troops to advance up the bluffs. Subsequently, by 0905 hrs, some 590 American troops had also managed to fight themselves off Dog (White) into the bluffs.

Despite incurring 1,020 casualties and pouring in reinforcements, by noon the four tiny American footholds on Omaha remained precarious. Just prior to this, FUSA Commander Omar Bradley had come close to ordering the forces landed to re-embark on to their transport vessels. In the west, between WN-70 and WN-68 at the Les Moulins (D-3) Draw, 116th RCT troops had secured a small salient.

FOOTHOLD

From here, several platoons had worked their way southwest to bring the inland end of the D-1 Vierville Draw, behind WN-71 and WN-72, under fire. In the west-centre, east of Les Moulins, along Dog (Green) and Easy (Red), the attackers also now held a small salient; from here, troops had pushed southeast to reach the inland end of the D-3 (Saint-Laurent) Draw.

PA26-15
LCVP PA26-15 from the transport USS *Samuel Chase* (APA-26) approaches Omaha Beach on D-Day; after being hit by enemy fire, smoke billows from the craft.

ABOVE:
READY FOR ACTION
American troops in a LCVP approach Omaha Beach on D-Day; with their personal weapons slung over their shoulders, they sport helmets with netting for the insertion of foliage as camouflage.

LEFT:
THE FALLEN
An American soldier lies dead alongside a German obstacle at Omaha Beach; by his feet, an M1 Garand semi-automatic rifle lies on the sand, with a M1903 Springfield bolt-action rifle laid across it.

OPPOSITE:
CAPTURED EMPLACEMENT
American troops move through a fortified installation within one of the German Resistance Nests along Omaha Beach that they had just secured; in the foreground lies the body of a dead German soldier.

GETTING OFF THE BEACH
At Omaha Beach sometime during 8 June 1944, long columns of newly arrived American soldiers march uphill inland off the beach and towards the front line; offshore, many dozens of Allied vessels are visible lying at anchor.

SUPPLIES AND REINFORCEMENTS
At Omaha during 7 June, two American LSTs, with their front double-doors wide open, lie beached in the shallows having disgorged their vehicular cargoes; above, numerous barrage balloons protect the fleet from enemy air attack.

ABOVE:
SHERMAN TANK
In the aftermath of the assault, wrecked Allied vehicles litter Omaha
Beach. In the forefront is a knocked-out Sherman tank that has shed
its left-hand track; behind it sit destroyed jeeps and other soft-
skinned vehicles.

BEACH SCENE
Dead lie on stretchers awaiting burial while piles of supplies litter the area on Omaha Beach. LCVP P77-7, from the auxiliary transport USS *Thurston* (APA-77), is in the foreground, while behind and to its right is American LCT US-638.

RHINO FERRY AND TUG BOAT
Out front, American Rhino tug RHT-3 assists the heavily laden powered Rhino ferry RHF-3 as it approaches the shore on D-Day. Note the name "Hell's Angels" painted across the tug's conning station shields.

In the centre-right, between the E-1 and E-3 Draws, 16th RCT troops had secured another enclave; from here, several combat teams had pushed south to close on Colleville. Finally in the east, along Fox, other 16th RCT troops had secured a small beachhead that included WN-60. From here, platoons had pushed south to Cabourg and southeast to Le Grand Hameau.

DISPOSITIONS AT NOON

The American position had improved, but these precarious embryonic beachheads remained vulnerable. By noon, the forces landed on Omaha were slowly wresting the beachhead away from looming failure. During that morning, the largely unsuppressed enemy defences had poured accurate machine-gun and rifle fire, augmented by mortar and artillery rounds, on to the beach. This hail of metal devastated the US infantry caught exposed on the beach.

In small part, the fact that by noon success at Omaha was beginning to drive away looming failure owed something to the relentless naval gunfire poured into the enemy defences. It also owed a little to the Allied invasion forces' mass, as wave after wave of reinforcements arrived at the beach. But mostly, this saving of the day was due to a few dozen courageous US soldiers. These brave troops managed to continue

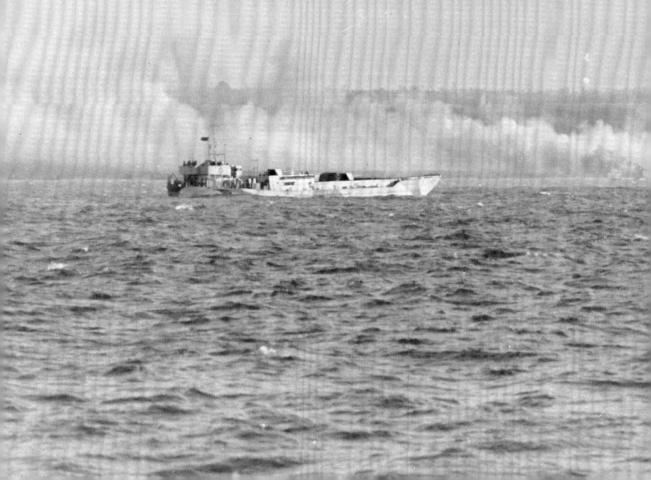

striving to achieve their mission amidst some of the most apocalyptic battlefield scenes ever witnessed. They somehow rallied the scared, confused and shell-shocked men around them, inspiring, cajoling or coercing them into action and persuading them to rouse themselves out of shell-scrapes and hollows and fight their way off the beach, into the dunes and off into the interior. Their actions saved the landings on Omaha Beach, when they lay on a knife-edge, staring into the abyss of failure.

This courage was all the more astonishing given that German fire had devastated the first assault-infantry waves, such as the 116th RCT's "A" Company on Dog (Green). Having reached the beach at 0636 hrs, within 12 minutes, all of "A" Company's officers and NCOs had been killed or wounded. Moreover, by 0706 hrs, some 65 per cent of "A" Company had become casualties, with many more temporarily incapacitated. Yet a few leaderless survivors somehow managed to fight on. Indeed, inspired by an "A" Company private taking the lead, by 0921 hrs, a group of six "A" Company Other Ranks had reached the bottom of the cliffs and begun climbing them. They were by then the only "A" Company element that still remained combat cohesive. Four of these soldiers, however, failed to complete the difficult climb due to exhaustion.

PREVIOUS PAGES:
CASUALTY EVACUATION
View taken late on 6 June from a large troop transport vessel as an LCM comes alongside; the latter is evacuating American casualties from an invasion beach. Three casualties with arm wounds sport slings.

BELOW:
SUPPORT ROLE
LCG(L)-429 and LCG(L)-424 stand offshore in support of landing operations at Omaha Beach, 6 June 1944. Armed with 120mm (4.7in) QF guns, these were British Landing Craft, Gun (Large) borrowed by the US Navy for shore bombardment duties.

The remaining two – Privates Shefer and Lovejoy – worked their way inland and linked up with US 2nd Rangers' soldiers who had landed on the adjacent Charlie Sector.

These troops fixed the defenders of WN-72 in contact, which to an extent facilitated other US troops further east to move inland to reach the interior end of the D-1 Draw, thereby outflanking both WN-71 and WN-72.

CONCLUSIONS

The task of establishing beachheads at Utah and Omaha had been made challenging by the marshes behind the former, the bluffs at the latter and the large geographical obstacle between them.

At Utah Beach, the combination of weak enemy defences, accurate preliminary bombardments and US paratrooper actions inland ensured that by midnight a sizeable beachhead had been established without severe casualties being incurred.

At Omaha, meanwhile, follow-up troops had pushed further inland from the tentative territorial gains made by noon. Indeed, by midnight, 34,100 Allied troops had landed on Omaha, of which 2,410 had become casualties. That afternoon, US forces had pushed the defenders of the D-1 (Vierville) Draw back to its western flanks and also secured the D-3 (Saint-Laurent) Draw. American forces had also both pushed 1.6km (1 mile) south through the E-1 Draw and forced the defenders of the E-3 Draw back to Colleville.

The Omaha beachhead was still precarious, but probably now had enough depth to ensure that any German ripostes during 7 June could not drive the invaders back into the sea. By midnight, the two American beachheads also had sufficient depth that newly landed US forces could rapidly expand them in the ensuing days.

BRADLEY AND KIRK
Senior US officers watching operations from the bridge of USS *Augusta* (CA-31), off Normandy, 8 June 1944. They are (from left to right): Rear Admiral Alan G. Kirk, USN, Commander Western Naval Task Force; Lieutenant General Omar N. Bradley, Commanding General, US First Army; Rear Admiral Arthur D. Struble, USN (with binoculars) Chief of Staff for RAdm. Kirk; and Major General Ralph Royce, US Army.

LSTS ON THE BEACH
A row of at least 11 American Landing Ships, Tank (LSTs) lie beached on Omaha; from them, many dozens of soft-skinned vehicles carrying logistical supplies are in the process of disembarking into the shallows and thence across the sandy beach.

THE BRITISH AND CANADIAN BEACHES

As the US beach assaults unfolded, further east, Lt-Gen Miles Dempsey's Second British Army simultaneously mounted its own three beach assaults on (from west to east) Gold, Juno and Sword beaches. The sector across which these three beaches stretched ran for 37km (23 miles) from Port-en-Bessin in the west through to Ouistreham and the River Orne in the east. On Gold Beach, the spearhead of Lt-Gen Gerard Bucknall's British XXX Corps landed. Meanwhile, across Dempsey's central and eastern sectors, at Juno and Sword beaches, the vanguards of Lt-Gen John Crocker's I Corps mounted their assaults. A 15km (9 mile) gap existed between Omaha, the eastern US beach, and Gold, the western Anglo-Canadian beach.

By midnight on 6 June, the Anglo-Canadian forces landed on these three beaches were slated to have linked up with one another, as well as with the Omaha beachhead in the west and the British airborne bridgehead in the west. If these objectives had been met, the landings at Omaha, Gold, Juno and Sword beaches would have formed a continuous 71km (44 mile)-wide beachhead out to a maximum depth of 18km (11 miles); in the process, the towns of Bayeux and Caen would have been captured.

OPPOSITE:
ROYAL MARINE COMMANDOS MOVE INLAND
Heavily laden soldiers from 45 (Royal Marine) Commando, part of 1st Special Service Brigade (which had been attached to the 3rd Infantry Division for D-Day), move inland from Sword Beach during the morning of 6 June.

BEACH CONTROL PARTIES
British beach control soldiers (identified by the white horizontal band around their helmets) and medics (with white arm-bands) attend to a number of lightly wounded comrades on Gold Beach.

GOLD BEACH

The western Anglo-Canadian beach, Gold, stretched for 14.5km (9 miles) from Port-en-Bessin in the west through to La Rivière in the east. The Allies divided this beach into four sub-sectors; from west to east, How, Item, Jig and King. However, offshore rocks that were exposed at low tide meant that the amphibious assault was restricted to Jig and King. The reinforced British veteran 50th (Northumbrian) Infantry Division executed the landings on Gold. Between 0545 and 0728 hrs, five Allied cruisers, 13 destroyers and four LCT-Rs bombarded the German defences, augmented by the 50th Division's 72 ship-borne artillery pieces.

This deluge was reinforced by strikes mounted by 136 fighter-bombers and 258 American B-17 heavy bombers. Gold was defended by elements of the German 352nd (field) Infantry Division, which included under command attached units from the 716th Division's 726th Grenadier Regiment. These forces manned 16 Resistance Nests, including WN-33 La Rivière in the east, as well as WN-37 and WN-38 at Le Hamel in the centre. On the western flank of Gold was the Longues-sur-Mer artillery battery that housed four 15.5cm (6.1in) guns.

AMPHIBIOUS ASSAULT BEGINS

At 0725 hrs, the 50th Division's amphibious assault began. Deployed offshore were Assault Groups G1, G2 and G3, which deployed between them eight LSIs, 24 LSTs, 151 LCTs, four LCT-Rs and 145 LCAs. On Jig, the forward two infantry battalions of the 231st Brigade Group, reinforced by 47 Royal

DISEMBARKING

50th Division infantry disembark on to Gold Beach past a Sexton; this self-propelled gun was based on the Sherman M4A1 chassis and mounted in a fixed superstructure of a Royal Ordnance QF 25-pounder (87.6 mm, 3.45in) Mark II field gun.

LEFT:
GO!
This grainy close-up photograph depicts the backs of a group of British infantry; the half-turned face of the soldier on the right understandably betrays anxiety, for the ensuing minutes would be riddled with extreme danger.

OPPOSITE:
THUMBS UP
Royal Marine Commandos equipped with their trademark Bergen rucksacks give the thumbs up after landing at Gold Beach.

BELOW:
PRIMING GRENADES
An NCO from 45 (Royal Marine) Commando primes a No. 36 Hand Grenade in readiness for the assault on Gold Beach. These lemon-shaped weapons – known as Mills bombs – weighed 0.9kg (2lb) and had a four-second delay.

Marine (RM) Commando, began to disembark from their LCAs into treacherous, fiercely swelling, chest-deep seawater.

Simultaneously, further west, the 69th Brigade Group's first-wave infantry began their assault on King. Landed alongside the first infantry waves were the armoured breaching teams, which deployed between them 76 amphibious DD Shermans, 26 mine-clearing Sherman Crab Flails, 40 bunker-busting AVsRE, 32 RM Centaur close-support tanks and six armoured bulldozers. The rough sea condition, however, meant that the DD Shermans could not be disembarked there; instead, their LCTs had to bring them right up on to the shoreline for disembarkation.

NAVAL BOMBARDMENT

The accurate preliminary Allied naval and aerial bombardments effectively suppressed most of the German defences, enabling the lead infantry waves to get ashore, cross the beach and begin pushing inland within the first 45 minutes without suffering catastrophic casualties.

The exception to this effective suppression was Le Hamel strongpoint, consisting of Resistance Nests WN-37 and WN-38. The preliminary fire directed at Le Hamel failed to score direct hits, leaving the enemy defenders manning their weapons as the assault infantry attempted to cross the western half of Jig.

Moreover, with fewer than expected specialized AFVs arriving on time opposite Le Hamel, several 1st Hampshire platoons became pinned down by intense enemy fire. Subsequent advances inland on both flanks helped the British mount repeated assaults on Le Hamel, which resisted fiercely before being overrun by 1605 hrs.

In the meantime, on King Beach, the 6th Green Howards had successfully pushed inland from La Rivière to overrun the Mont Fleury Battery, with its six 122mm (4.8in) ex-Soviet artillery pieces, by 0930 hrs. By late morning, furthermore, the 69th Brigade's lead elements, landed on King, had cleared the entire area of Ver-sur-Mer. During the rest of the morning, 50th Division's units continued to widen and deepen the beachhead established at Gold.

DEPLOYING ARMOUR
During the mid-afternoon of D-Day, the US Coast Guard-manned LST US-21, located off Jig (Green) Sector at Gold Beach, unloaded on to Rhino ferry F-100 the 73 vehicles (and their 220 crew) it had transported from Southampton; a British Sherman is in the foreground.

JUNO BEACH

Located centrally within the Anglo-Canadian invasion sector, Juno stretched eastwards for 10km (6 miles) from near La Rivière, the extreme right (eastern) flank of Gold Beach. Juno Sector then ran eastwards through Courseulles-sur-Mer and on to Saint-Aubin-sur-Mer in the east. The Allies divided this beach into three sub-sectors, designated (from west to east) as Love, Mike and Nan. The sub-sector Love stretched for 1.9km (1 mile) from La Rivière to opposite Hameau de Vaux, while Mike ran from the latter through to Courseulles' harbour. Finally, Nan Sector stretched east for 4km (2 miles) to Saint-Aubin-sur-Mer.

Juno Beach, like Sword Beach to the east, came under the control of Lt-Gen John Crocker's I (British) Corps. The formation allocated the task of assaulting Juno was the 3rd Canadian Infantry Division, the primary Canadian land contingent involved in D-Day. Elements of the German 716th Division defended this sector, with its subordinated 736th Grenadier Regiment manning nine coastal Resistance Nests.

As with the other beaches, during 0550–0748 hrs, naval and aerial bombardments softened up and suppressed the German defences. Meanwhile, at sea, the transport vessels of Naval Assault Group J – 10 LSIs, 24 LSTs, 92 LCTs, 8 LCT-Rs and 131 LCAs – began their designated entry runs to the shoreline. Finally, at 0750 hrs, the 7th Canadian Infantry Brigade's amphibious assault commenced on Mike and Nan (Green) between La Rivière and Courseulles. Simultaneously, the 8th Canadian Infantry Brigade, later augmented by 48 RM Commando, mounted its landings on Nan (White) and Nan (Red) sectors east of Courseulles.

As the lead echelon of 84 LCAs reached the shoreline, LCTs manoeuvred close in to disgorge their specialized AFVs on to the beach. As with the other beaches, this force included DD Shermans, Crab Flails, AVsRE, Centaurs and bulldozers. At Juno, the storm had again pushed the incoming tide higher than the Allies had calculated, with the result that a number of the LCAs hit underwater obstacles they had expected to still be visible above the waterline.

ANGLO-CANADIAN ADVANCE INLAND

Subsequently, by 0925 hrs, the lead elements of both brigades had secured their adjacent beach sectors. Thereafter, the 3rd Canadian Division's spearheads began to advance inland. That morning, along the 3rd Division's western flank, 7th Brigade's vanguards pushed forwards on four axes: due west along the coast road to La Rivière (where they linked up with British 50th Division spearheads); 3km (1.9 miles) southwest to reach the northern approaches to Sainte-Croix-sur-Mer; 2km (1.2 miles)

OPPOSITE ABOVE:
GERMAN POWS
While a British Corporal directs proceedings, a British 50th Division soldier encourages with his rifle two German prisoners-of-war – their hands held high above their heads – to move forwards to a secure reception area on Gold Beach, 6 June 1944.

OPPOSITE BELOW:
APPROACHING JUNO
A column of at least five LCAs, with each craft carrying a platoon from the Royal Winnipeg Rifles, from Brigadier H.W. Foster's Canadian 7th Infantry Brigade (part of 3rd Division), approach the shore at Mike Sector, Juno Beach.

south to Banville; and east along the coast into the western fringes of the fiercely defended town of Courseulles.

Meanwhile, the 8th Canadian Brigade's vanguards had pushed 3.8km (2.4 miles) south towards Bény-sur-Mer. Other 8th Brigade units had also advanced south-southeast into the fringes of Saint-Aubin-sur-Mer. The enemy forces defending parts of the small towns of Courseulles and Saint-Aubin, however, fought determinedly and Allied forces made slow progress in both locations that morning.

SWORD BEACH

The eastern Anglo-Canadian beach, termed "Sword", stretched for 13km (8 miles) from Saint-Aubin-sur-Mer in the west through to the River Orne estuary at Ouistreham in the east. A 3.2km (2 mile)-wide gap separated the landings on Sword from its neighbour to the west, Juno. The Allies had divided Sword into four sectors; from west to east, Oboe, Peter, Queen and Roger. A long range of offshore rocks, visible at low tide, however, prevented the invasion forces from assaulting Oboe and Peter sectors. The British 3rd Division – the spearhead force of Lt-Gen Crocker's I (British) Corps – was to mount the assault on Sword. The 3rd Division's vanguard force – the reinforced 8th Brigade Group – constituted the first assault wave; its operations centred primarily on Queen.

CANADIAN ASSAULT

At 0755 hrs on D-Day, first-wave assault infantry from the 3rd Canadian Infantry Division disembark from their LCAs into swirling, waist-deep seas; soft focus in the distance in the photo are two of the seafront houses that the Germans had heavily fortified.

LOSING BALANCE
Commandos from the British 4th Special Service Brigade's HQ disembark from LCI(S)-536 on Nan (Red) Sector, Juno Beach; the soldier in the centre, apparently manoeuvring a bicycle, has been photographed in the process of falling into the sea.

BICYCLE TROOPS
Follow-on troops of 9th Canadian Infantry Brigade, from the Highland Light Infantry of Canada, disembark with bicycles into waist-deep water at high tide from the Canadian LCI(L) HMC-255 on to Nan (White) Sector, Juno Beach just before noon on D-Day.

ADVANCING OFF THE BEACH
Canadian infantry take shelter by a low ridge of scrub just off Juno Beach, ready to continue the advance inland; the platoon commander (foreground) sports a Sten submachine gun and on his back, an entrenching tool.

ABOVE:
LORD LOVAT
An iconic image, taken at 0840 hrs on D-Day, depicts 1st Special Service Brigade Commandos, directed by Brigadier Lord Lovat (in the water to the right of the line of troops) disembarking at Queen (Red) Sector, Sword Beach; 13th/18th Royal Hussar DD Shermans are already on the beach.

OPPOSITE TOP:
FLAIL TANK ADVANCES
In the centre, a Sherman Crab flail mine-clearing tank advances towards the camera across the smoke-ridden, muddy flats of Sword Beach. To the left of the Sherman is a Churchill 'carpet-laying' tank, designed to provide a roadway over soft ground for armoured fighting vehicles.

OPPOSITE BELOW:
CHURCHILL AVRE
Sitting on Sword Beach is a Churchill AVRE (left), armed with its bunker-busting Petard spigot mortar; on the right is a US-designed M10 tank destroyer – officially designated as the 3-Inch Motor Gun Carriage M10.

QUEEN (RED) SECTOR
0800 hrs, 6 June 1944: Sherman tanks from the 13th/18th Royal Hussars (Queen Mary's Own) can be seen through the smoke on Queen (Red) Sector, Sword Beach, from LCT 610.

The sector of the Normandy coast on which Sword lay was defended by the German 716th (static) Infantry Division. The sector designated as Queen was protected by elements of the 736th Grenadier Regiment, which manned five strongpoints, including that at La Brèche. Finally, the three northernmost units of the 21st Panzer Division, the Seventh Army's reserve, were located across the northern approaches to Caen, 4.8km (3 miles) inland from Ouistreham.

At Sword, the landings were also preceded by aerial and naval bombardments. Meanwhile, at 0715 hrs, the first LCA waves began their final approach to the beach. Here, the surge created by the storm had made the tide higher than expected. This meant that several landing craft hit concealed German underwater obstacles that the Allies had expected to be visible at the halfway mark of the incoming tide scheduled for 0725 hrs. This reality also reduced the depth of the beach, which eased the assault infantry's charge across the sandy killing ground to the sea wall. On the flip side, however, it made it much harder for follow-up forces' vehicles to manoeuvre off the congested narrow strip of beach. At 0726 hrs, the first wave of LCT-delivered specialized AFVs – Sherman

ABOVE:
WADING ASHORE
Three heavily laden soldiers of the 1st Battalion, the Royal Norfolk Regiment (from the British 3rd Division's 185th Infantry Brigade) struggle to wade through chest-high seas towards the shore at Sword Beach during the early morning of D-Day.

OPPOSITE:
BEACH CONTROL PARTIES
British beach control parties labour to bring some order to the chaotic scenes on Sword Beach during the afternoon of D-Day; just to the upper left of the soldier in the foreground, a dozer clears a pathway for AFVs to utilize.

Flails, Churchill AVREs and Centaurs – reached the beach. Next, 20 LCA-delivered first-wave infantry platoons reached the shoreline. Finally, at 0727 hrs, the first echelon of 28 amphibious DD Shermans disembarked on to the beach. Enemy artillery and heavy mortar fire landed close to these craft as they approached, but very few vessels received direct hits.

By 0750 hrs, the 1st South Lancs and 2nd East Yorks were established ashore and fighting themselves forward, supported by whatever specialized armour had arrived. Subsequently, by 0815 hrs, the two battalions had fought themselves off the beach, having secured four exits.

OPPOSITE ABOVE:
DISABLED DD SHERMAN
A British Sherman DD amphibious tank from the 4th/7th Royal
Dragoon Guards has become bogged down in a depression on
Sword Beach, quite possibly a shell crater; note that its canvas screen
floatation skirt has been disassembled.

OPPOSITE BELOW:
MARCHING INLAND
On the late morning of D-Day, soldiers of 4 Commando (part of 1st
Special Service Brigade), march through a hamlet south of Sword
Beach en route to relieve Major Howard's airborne troops that had
seized "Pegasus" Bridge; this juncture was achieved at 1330 hrs.

ABOVE:
UNIVERSAL CARRIERS
Universal Carriers from the 2nd Middlesex Regiment (3rd Division's
Machine Gun Battalion) move inland from Queen (White) Sector,
Sword Beach, through the main street of La Brèche d'Hermanville
past a Churchill AVRE tank.

1ST SPECIAL SERVICES BRIGADE

Two platoon-sized groups of 1st Special Service Brigade troops
advance at the double from Sword Beach into the interior; they
would seem to be carrying significant weight, judging by their large
and bulging Bergen rucksacks.

Subsequently, additional waves of landing craft delivered the first reinforcement echelons from 185th Infantry Brigade on to Sword Beach. As elsewhere, these vessels disgorged numerous troops and vehicles on to the ever-narrowing sand of the beach as high tide approached. Soon, a large traffic jam had emerged, which hampered the movement of forces inland. Despite this, by 1105 hrs, the 185th Brigade's infantry and soft-skinned vehicles had managed to form up inland around Hermanville. However, their supporting tanks were absent, having been delayed by the traffic congestion on the beach.

At noon, having wasted an hour waiting in vain for the tanks to arrive, the brigade's two lead battalions advanced inland regardless; the supporting armour was to catch up as best it could. During that morning, the British invasion forces had incurred 396 casualties establishing the initial beachhead on Sword.

AFTERNOON EXPLOITATION

At Gold beachhead during the afternoon of D-Day, the British 50th Division pushed forwards against variable enemy resistance. Nevertheless, by dusk on 6 June, the westernmost element landed on Gold – 47 RM Commando – had pushed west to close on Port-en-Bessin. Simultaneously, the 50th Division's western elements – 56th Brigade – had advanced 8km (5 miles) southwest to capture Vaux-sur-Aure and Saint-Sulpice, just shy of the key town of Bayeux. In the division's centre, meanwhile, 151st Brigade's spearheads had pushed south to capture by evening Esquay-sur-Seulles, located 4km (2.5 miles) west of Bayeux. Simultaneously, along the 50th Division's eastern flank, the 69th Brigade advanced southeast to link up with the southwesterly advance of 3rd Canadian Division units that had landed at Juno. The 69th Brigade's spearheads then pushed south-southwest a further 10km (6 miles) to close by nightfall on Coulombs, some 12km (7.5 miles)

inland. By nightfall, a total of 20,400 Allied troops had disembarked on to Norman soil via Gold Beach. During D-Day, the 50th Division and its attached forces suffered 708 casualties, with a further 156 being incurred by the maritime or aerial forces employed in this invasion sector.

Meanwhile, during the afternoon, 3rd Canadian Division units continued to press inland from Juno. The shallower than expected beach at high tide here, as elsewhere, was an obstacle to faster exploitation as the traffic congestion slowed the movement of reinforcements towards the frontline. Nevertheless, that afternoon, in the west, 7th Brigade's forces pushed southwest to Cruelly and south to Le-Fresne-Camilly, some 7km (4.3 miles) inland. Around Cruelly, moreover, Canadian infantry linked up with the British 69th Brigade, which had landed on Gold. Simultaneously, other 7th Brigade units advanced south-southeast to Fontaine-Henry. Meanwhile, in the east, 8th Brigade units pushed south-southeast to Anguerny and Anisy. Finally, on the division's northeastern flank, 48 RM Commando meanwhile cleared Saint-Aubin in the face of fierce resistance.

For the cost of 1,210 ground force casualties, the 21,400 troops landed on Juno on D-Day had secured by midnight a 7km (4.3 mile)-wide by 8km (5 mile)-deep beachhead. As the Juno beachhead had by midnight also joined up with the eastern flank of the Gold beachhead, this created a large contiguous salient stretching 19km (12 miles) from west to east and from up to 9.5km (6 miles) north to south.

During the early afternoon at Sword, the British 1st Special Service Brigade continued to advance south-southeast towards the positions held by British 6th Airborne Division east of the Orne. At 1335 hrs, the 1st Brigade's lead commandos reached Bénouville and took over the defences manned by Howard's troops at "Pegasus" Bridge; other commandos then pushed on to link up with 9 Para south of Merville Battery.

ABOVE:
STRETCHER BEARERS
During the afternoon of D-Day, four British soldiers, probably Royal Marine commandos, between them carry a wounded comrade on a stretcher back to an aid post; despite the physical effort involved, two of the stretcher party are still each smoking a cigarette.

LEFT:
GETTING OFF THE BEACH
A column of Allied vehicles – including a DUKW amphibious truck – drive south of Juno Beach, in the vicinity of Saint-Aubin-sur-Mer, during the afternoon of 6th June 1944.

NAVAL GUN FIRE OBSERVERS
From inland on 7 June, a three-man Forward Observer Bombardment team directs naval gun fire support delivered by some of the Allied warships stationed off the Normandy coast; the binocular-utilizing sergeant (right) sports a Thompson submachine gun.

Meanwhile, 185th Brigade's spearheads continued to push south that afternoon to reach Biéville. Further east, as 41 Commando attacked Lion-sur-Mer, the British 8th and 9th Brigades thrust southwest.

The bitter resistance offered by WN-17 (Hillman), south of Colleville-Montgomery, initially stalled their drive south on to the Périers Ridge. This setback enabled 21st Panzer Division units to advance north towards the coast through the gap that existed between the Sword and Juno beachheads. Fierce resistance by the British units that had just reached the Périers Ridge, however, eventually forced the German armour to withdraw. By midnight, therefore, the 28,845 Allied troops landed on Sword had, for the price of 883 casualties, linked up with the 6th Airborne Division's beachhead to create a salient that was 15km (9 miles) wide by up to 11km (7 miles) deep.

ENEMY ARMOURED RESPONSES

The enemy's armoured reserves posed the gravest threat to the nascent D-Day beachheads. Their early commitment on 6 June may have offered the enemy their only chance of throwing the invaders back into the sea, although massed Allied naval fires would have inflicted catastrophic losses upon them. Allied deception efforts, however, had fooled many senior German commanders into believing that any invasion outside the Pas-de-Calais was a feint designed to draw in the panzer reserves before the "real" invasion occurred elsewhere. The reserve deployed closest to the invasion beaches, the 21st Panzer Division, was deployed dispersed across territory that stretched from north of Caen down to Falaise.

GUARDING POWS
The 5th Royal Berkshires – part of the tri-service No. 2 Beach (Control) Group – landed on Nan Sector, Juno Beach; here, close to enemy strongpoint WN-28, two of its soldiers guard captured German prisoners-of-war while others assist Allied walking wounded.

LEFT:
BEACH SCENE
Landing craft sit in the water
off Juno Beach as Allied troops
attempt to bring a semblance of
order to the landing zone. Note
the abandoned life jackets in the
left of the frame.

OPPOSITE TOP:
KNOCKED OUT
Allied tank crew and
American photographers
examine a damaged M4
Sherman Crab flail tank,
probably disabled by a mine
after advancing inland from
the beach.

It was only late on the morning of 6 June that Seventh Army released the 21st Panzer Division to LXXXIV Corps' control. The division's dispersed elements moved northwards, some of them travelling precariously through bombed-out Caen. Late that afternoon, a 21st Division battlegroup advanced north from Caen into the gap that existed between the Sword and Juno beachheads towards the sea. Eventually, furious British fire from the Périers Ridge forced the Germans back. The only significant armoured riposte the Germans managed on D-Day ended without achieving any success.

The early commitment against the embryonic D-Day beachheads, however, of two other elite German mobile reserves might have posed a yet more severe threat to the success of the Allied landings. The first was the Panzer Lehr Division, then deployed south of the line from Le Mans to Chartres, at least 147km (91 miles) from Ouistreham. The second was the 12th SS Panzer Division Hitlerjugend, then located between Argentan and Elbeuf, some 74km (46 miles) as the crow flies from Ouistreham. Both divisions were designated as German High Command (OKW) strategic reserves. They could thus only be activated to move towards the invasion by a direct order from the German Führer, Adolf Hitler.

Both the OKW and Panzer Group West, however, believed in the importance of preserving their best strategic armoured reserves until it had definitely established that any Allied invasion was the real thing and not a feint. Consequently, it was not until mid-afternoon on D-Day that both divisions were released to the Seventh Army. While some of these divisions' units managed to begin moving forwards that evening, many others only did so under the shroud of darkness. However, by then it was already too late for the counter-attack they were instructed to launch on 7 June to successfully throw the invaders back into the sea.

CONCLUSIONS

Although the Allies had made astonishing efforts to ensure that the five D-Day amphibious and two airborne assaults were successful, the actions waged that day were still very risky, and descent into disaster was not impossible. That said, with the exception of Omaha, the other beach assaults had achieved significant success, albeit with high casualties (but not as high as the Allies had anticipated). By midnight on 6 June, the Allies had got 159,000 troops ashore in Normandy – 24,000 by air and 135,000 across the beaches.

The Allied amphibious assaults had successfully established four sizeable beachheads, and one precarious one at Omaha. The forces that had assaulted Sword had linked up with the 6th Airborne to create a large salient, while the forces landed at Juno and Gold had also joined up; further west came the two American beachheads.

Although the embryonic invasion front remained vulnerable to enemy ripostes, the stunning success achieved on D-Day now made it extraordinarily challenging for the Germans to repel the Allied attack. The successful establishment of the Second Front on 6 June represented a vital waypoint on the gradual Allied journey to strategic victory over Hitler's Reich.

LEFT:
BERNIÈRES-SUR-MER
Canadian troops from the Queen's Own Rifles hold up a French tricolour following the capture of Bernières on the afternoon of 6 June. They are being recorded by an American film crew.

AFTERMATH

During 7–9 June, the Allies determinedly pushed inland before the panzer divisions could arrive en masse. During the ensuing weeks, however, fierce enemy resistance significantly slowed the Allied advance. With the campaign degenerating into attrition, the Allies regularly mounted offensives that merely accomplished modest gains. During 25–31 July, however, the American Operation Cobra offensive around Saint-Lô in the west achieved a decisive breakthrough. With the German front torn asunder, during 1–6 August, American forces raced west into Brittany, south towards the Loire and east towards the Seine against minimal resistance.

In response, German panzer forces struck west towards the coast at Avranches during 6–7 August, aiming to cut off the American forces then charging deep into central France. This failed riposte inadvertently pushed German forces west, deeper into an encirclement that was forming in the Mortain–Argentan area. For at the same time, in the east, British and Canadian offensives had meanwhile closed on Falaise during 8–15 August.

Subsequently, the German Seventh Army was encircled and all but destroyed in the Falaise Pocket during 17–21 August. The remaining German forces then skilfully withdrew behind the Seine. By 28 August,

OPPOSITE:
LIBERATION!
Men of 46 (Royal Marine) Commando, 4th Special Service Brigade, are watched by French civilians as they enter the village of Douvres-la-Délivrande, 8 June 1944.

therefore, the Allies had completed the clearance of all French territory located north of the Loire and east of the Seine; the Allies had decisively won the crucial Battle for Normandy.

NEW FRONTLINE

Subsequently, the Allied forces continued to charge north through Belgium and east towards the German border during 1–10 September. By then, other Allied forces had landed in southern France, forcing the Germans to retreat north until they reached the western approaches to Alsace–Lorraine.

By mid-September, however, the defending German forces were swiftly regaining their cohesion. Thus, on 17 September, the Allies launched the "Market Garden" offensive to secure a bridge over the Rhine at Arnhem. The offensive's failure forced the Allies during October–November to wage grinding attritional advances north through the Netherlands' southern fringes and east towards the Siegfried Line defences on Germany's western border.

On 16 December, however, the Germans initiated a surprise counter-offensive in the Ardennes. Having defeated this enemy riposte, between January and early March 1945, the Allies gradually advanced towards the Rhine. During March, Allied offensives secured bridgeheads across the Rhine, and their forces charged east deep into German territory. By 25 April, the eastward American advance had linked up with the Soviet Army's westward advance at the River Elbe. Finally, on 8 May, the defeated German forces signed a strategic unconditional surrender: the Allies had won World War II in Europe.

INTERROGATION

On 15 June 1944, somewhere within the Allied bridgehead, American soldiers interrogate a German soldier of Polish ethnicity; during 1943–44, the Germans forcibly conscripted 90,000 ethnic Poles. Taken by Combat Photo Unit Eleven (CPU-11).

AFTERMATH

ABOVE:
NORMANDY *BOCAGE*
An M4 Sherman tank advances
along a track carved through the
densely overgrown lanes of the
Normandy *bocage*; note how the
crew have draped foliage across its
turret front as camouflage.

RIGHT:
GENERALS CONFER
British General Bernard Law
Montgomery (second from right)
in discussion with several British
officers and a smiling Lieutenant-
General George Patton (left),
the commander of the Third
US Army. This photograph, and
the one opposite, were taken at
21st Army Group HQ on
7 July 1944, just a month after
the landings.

218

ABOVE:
NORMAN VILLAGE
A soft-skinned US Army truck transports a dozen or so American soldiers along a Norman village street. The damaged buildings are in typical Norman style: tall, thick-walled and with many windows that the enemy could buttress and use as firing positions.

LEFT:
MEDAL CEREMONY
General Montgomery, commander of the 21st Army Group and temporary ground forces theatre commander, pins a decoration on the chest of an American paratrooper from the 101st Airborne Division.

LANDING REINFORCEMENTS
Long after D-Day had passed, many Allied landing craft remained grounded in the shallows where they had beached themselves that day. Here, South Saskatchewan Regiment infantry, from 2nd Canadian Infantry Division, walk across Juno Beach after being landed, 8 July 1944.

LEGACY
At Arromanches-les-Bains today, parts of the former
Mulberry harbour built on Gold Beach can be seen lying
on the sand at low tide, with remains of Phoenix caissons
in the distance.

Picture Credits

Airsealand.Photos: 11, 14 top, 19 top, 22-25, 28/29, 30/31, 38/39, 41 bottom, 42 bottom, 44/45, 48/49, 50, 53 bottom, 61, 62 top, 63 both, 66/67, 70 both, 72/73, 81 top, 84-86, 90-98, 10/103, 105, 106/107, 110-117, 122/123, 124, 138/139, 140, 141 top, 142 both, 143 top, 146-155, 156 bottom, 161-163, 180-183, 187 both, 190/191, 196-207 top, 208/209

Alamy: 43 (dpa picture alliance), 46 top (Everett Collection Historical), 52, 54 bottom & 55 bottom (TT News Agency), 210/211 (Shawshots)

Dreamstime: 222/223 (Olrat)

Getty Images: 14 bottom (Reg Speller/Fox Photos), 19 bottom (IWM), 20/21 (Popperfoto), 26/27 (Toronto Star Archives), 36 (AFP), 41 top (Roger Viollet), 42 top, 46 bottom & 53 top (Keystone-France), 54 top & 55 top (ullstein bild), 58/59 (Roger Viollet), 88/89 (FPG), 99 top (PhotoQuest), 99 bottom (Fred Ramage), 100/101 (Keystone), 108/109 & 118/119 (IWM), 120 (Education Images), 121 top (Bettmann), 121 bottom (PhotoQuest), 126/127 (U.S. Navy), 144/145 (Galerie Bilderwelt), 178/179 (Popperfoto), 188/189 (Galerie Bilderwelt), 192/193 (IWM), 194/195 & 214 (Popperfoto), 220/221 (Galerie Bilderwelt)

Library of Congress, Motion Picture, Broadcasting, and Recorded Sound Division: 7, 75 top, 81 bottom-83, 207 bottom, 212-213, 218-219

National Archives and Records Administration: 56, 62 bottom, 134/135, 157 top

Naval History and Heritage Command: 5, 8, 10 both, 12/13, 32/33, 34 both, 35, 64, 68/69, 71, 75 bottom-80, 128-133, 136/137, 141 bottom, 143 bottom, 156 top, 158, 160 both, 164-175, 184/185, 216/217

Public Domain: 6, 16/17, 51, 60, 176

U.S. Department of Defense: 104

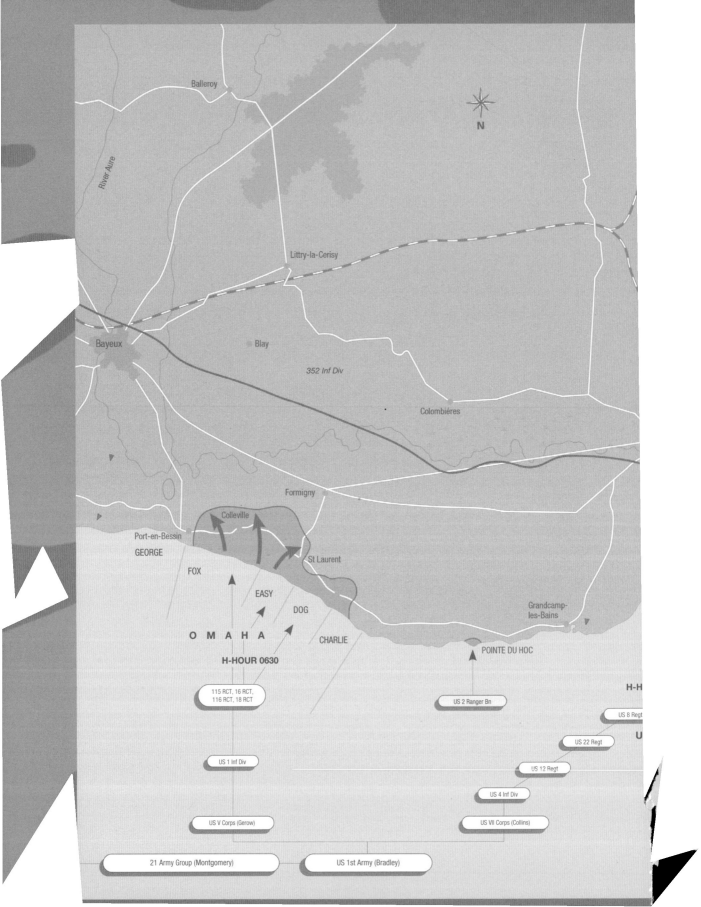

Balleroy

River Aure

Littry-la-Cerisy

Bayeux

Blay

352 Inf Div

Colombiéres

Formigny

Colleville

Port-en-Bessin

GEORGE

St Laurent

FOX

EASY

DOG

Grandcamp-
les-Bains

OMAHA

CHARLIE

POINTE DU HOC

H-HOUR 0630

115 RCT, 16 RCT,
116 RCT, 18 RCT

US 2 Ranger Bn

H-H

US 8 Regt

US 22 Regt

U

US 12 Regt

US 1 Inf Div

US 4 Inf Div

US V Corps (Gerow)

US VII Corps (Collins)

21 Army Group (Montgomery)

US 1st Army (Bradley)